"The people have a right to clean air, pure water, and to the preservation of the natural, scenic, historic, and aesthetic values of the environment. Pennsylvania's public natural resources are the common property of all the people, including generations yet to come. As trustees of these resources, the Commonwealth shall conserve and maintain them for the benefit of all the people."

Article 1, Section 27
Constitution of Pennsylvania

Mountain Bike Madness

Mountain Bike Madness in Central PA

AN ATLAS OF CENTRAL PENNSYLVANIA'S GREATEST MOUNTAIN BIKE RIDES

BY
SCOTT ADAMS

Beachway Press

Cover design and illustrations by Walt Wait
Photographs taken by Harry Winand

Maps used in this book:
United States Geological Survey maps
Pennsylvania Public Use Maps

Library of Congress Catalog Card No. 93-70131
Adams, Scott
Mountain Bike Madness in Central PA
An Atlas of Central Pennsylvania's Greatest Mountain Bike Rides
ed. 1,
First Printing, 1993

ISBN 1-882997-02-6

Published by Beachway Press

Printed by Automated Graphics Systems
White Plains, Maryland
in the United States of America

This book is dedicated
to three restless cyclists
who brought mountain biking to the east coast.
If not them, then surely someone else:

Randy Moore, Jim Taylor, Tom Taylor

and the Bomber Club's *pioneering spirit*

Tons of thanks to:

Bill Hromyak and his inspiration
Harry Winand and all his smiles
Jim Bryant, Kim Cole, Tom Cross
Tony DeAngelo, Mark Okrand
Carolyn Pickering, Scott Ramsey
Anna Scharf, Mark Warno
All the great folks in the park service, especially the District Foresters
The friendly family at The Bicycle Shop
and of course, my fantastic family

CONTENTS

MID STATE TRAIL

INTRODUCTION

A trip to Shingletown Gap, near the small town of Boalsburg, will reveal the catastrophic results of overcrowding and congestion on a trailway. Once a quiet watershed, Shingletown Gap has become an overrated, muddy bog. Years of continuous riding, especially during the wet seasons, have been disastrous. Ironically, there are thousands of acres of state forest land and hundreds of miles of fire roads and trails in the Central Pennsylvania region that go virtually unused by bicyclists. I hope this guidebook will relieve the congestion of certain popular trails, while exposing new roads and trails more accommodating to both cyclists and other outdoors people.

The rides included in this book are by no means strictly confined courses dictating where you can and cannot ride; rather they are introductions to the backcountry, wide open to all the possibilities of Central Pennsylvania's state forests. Each ride should introduce you to a specific area, then send you off on your own adventures in search of other unique and beautiful places.

WHAT THIS BOOK IS ABOUT

Besides the great off-road rides you'll find in the following pages, *Mountain Bike Madness* explores the fascinating history of the mountain bike and reveals the *true* origins of the Central Pennsylvania region. Also included are diagrams of many common trees, shrubs, and animals you can expect to see, and three-dimensional profile maps to give you a better look at each ride. The controversy mountain bikes have created and the rules and etiquette that apply to this sport are also addressed, as are Pennsylvania's bicycling laws. There are even tips and techniques for off-road riding, important items to carry with you, and a sampling of some stylish gear to match the seasons.

Each ride highlights a small section of Central Pennsylvania's thousands of acres of natural beauty contained within its state forests. Many of these rides begin at popular state parks and travel in loops that are, for the most part, between 10 and 20 miles long. All rides avoid, as much as possible, using the same roads and trails more than once per ride.

It is important to know that mountain bike rides tend to take longer than road rides because the average speed is often much slower. Average speeds can vary from a walking pace of three to four miles an hour when climbing, to 12 or 13 miles an hour on flatter roads and trails. Keep this in mind when planning your trip.

Bike riding into the backcountry can be an incredibly enriching and enjoyable experience. I hope this book will tell you everything you need to know to enjoy this sport to its nearly unlimited potential.

MOUNTAIN BIKE BEGINNINGS

It seems that the mountain bike, originally designed for lunatic adventurists bored with straight-line riding and clean clothes, has become globally popular in as short a time as it would take to race down a mountain trail.

Like most things of a revolutionary nature, the mountain bike appears to have been born on the west coast. But unlike roller blades, purple hair, and the peace sign, the concept of the off-road bike cannot be credited solely to the imaginative Californians. They were just the first to make waves.

The design of the first off-road specific bikes was based on the geometry of the old Schwinn Excelsior, a one-speed, camel-back cruiser with balloon tires. Joe Breeze was the creator behind them, and in 1977 he built 10 of these "Breezers" for himself and his Marin County, California friends at $750 apiece -- a bargain.

Breeze was a serious competitor in bicycle racing, placing 13th in the 1977 U.S. road racing national championships. After races, he and friends would scour local bike shops hoping to find old bikes they could then restore.

It was the 1941 Schwinn Excelsior for which Breeze paid $5 that began to shape and change bicycling history forever. After taking the bike home, removing the fenders, oiling the chain, and pumping up the tires, Breeze hit the dirt and loved it.

His inspiration was not unique, though forerunning. On the opposite side of the country, nearly 2,500 miles from Marin County, bike bums on the east were also growing restless. More and more old beat-up clunkers were being restored and modified. These bikes often weighed nearly 80 pounds, and were so reinforced they seemed nearly indestructible. But many rides that take just 40 minutes on today's 25 pound bikes took the steel-toed-boot- and blue-jean-clad bikers of the late 1970s and early 1980s nearly four hours.

Not until 1981 was it possible to purchase a production mountain bike. These were rare, however, and local stores had yet to carry them in stock. By 1983, mountain bikes were no longer such a fringe item anymore, as larger bike manufacturers started producing their own versions of the off-road bike. By the 1990s, mountain bikes had found their place with bicyclists of nearly all ages and abilities, and they now command nearly 60% of the U.S. bike market.

For many reasons the mountain bike has become the hottest two-wheeled vehicle in the nation. They are much friendlier to the cyclist than traditional road bikes because of their comfortable upright position and fat tires. And because of the health-conscious, environmentalist generation of the late 1980s and 1990s, people have become more activity minded and more inclined to see nature first-hand and up close. The mountain bike allows for all these things, including a chance to get far away from everything.

MOUNTAIN BIKING INTO SHAPE

If your objective is to get in shape and lose weight, then you're on the right track because mountain biking is one of the best ways to get started.

One way many of us have lost weight is the crash-and-burn-it-off method. Picture this. Suddenly you're speeding uncontrollably down what seems to be a vertical drop. Your front wheel lodges into a canyon-like rut launching you into a horrific, flailing tumble for at least a half a mile. Through weeds, trees, and other painful objects you hurl until coming to rest in a puddle of thick mud. It is here where you discover that, with the layers of skin and body parts left behind during the crash, those unwanted pounds have been shed -- permanently. Instant weight loss.

There is, of course, the more conventional approach to losing weight and gaining fitness on a mountain bike. This is the physical workout you will get from riding. Take a look at the health benefits associated with cycling.

You don't need a trainer or a partner to ride a bike. Nor do you need to join a club or reserve a court. All you need is a bike and the desire to ride. You can enjoy a quiet bike ride alone or on a group ride with friends.

Cycling helps you shed pounds without gimmicky diet fads or weight-loss programs. You can explore the countryside and burn nearly 10-16 calories per minute or close to 600-1000 calories per hour. Just a fun way to spend an afternoon.

No less significant than the external and cosmetic changes in your body from riding are the internal changes taking place. Over time, cycling regularly can strengthen your heart as your body grows vast networks of new capillaries to carry blood to all the working muscles. This will, in turn, give your skin a healthier glow. The capacity of your lungs may increase up to 20% and your resting heart rate will drop significantly. In a report to the American Heart Association, Ralph S. Paffenburger, M.D., of the Stanford University School of Medicine; states that people can reduce their risk of heart attack by nearly 64% if they can burn up to 2000 calories per week. This is only two to three hours of bike riding!

Recommended for insomnia, hypertension, indigestion, anxiety, and even for recuperation from major heart attacks, bicycling can be an excellent cure-all as well as a great preventive. Cycling just a few hours a week can improve your figure and sleeping habits, give you greater resistance to illness, increase your energy levels, and give you a feeling of accomplishment and heightened self-esteem.

BE SAFE, KNOW THE LAW

Outlined below are a few of the laws in Pennsylvania's Vehicle Code book that are important for you to know and understand. (See Appendix B for a copy of the Pennsylvania Vehicle Code, chapter 35, subchapter A, Operation of Pedalcycles.)

- **Bicycles are legally classified as vehicles in the state of Pennsylvania**. This means that as a bicyclist you are responsible for obeying the same rules of the road as a driver of a motor vehicle.
- **Bicyclists must ride with the traffic (NOT AGAINST IT!)**. Because bicycles are considered vehicles, you must ride your bicycle just as you would drive a car -- with traffic. Only pedestrians should travel against the flow of traffic.
- **You must obey all traffic signs**. This includes stop signs and stop lights.
- **Always signal your turns**. Most drivers aren't expecting bicyclists to be on *their* roads, and many drivers would prefer that cyclists stay off the roads altogether. It is important, therefore, to let motorists behind or in front of you know your intentions, just as if you were driving.
- **Bicyclists are entitled to the same roads as cars**. (ie. controlled access highways). Unfortunately, however, cyclists are rarely given this consideration.
- **Be a responsible cyclist.** Do not abuse your rights to ride on open roads, and follow the rules. You can set a good example for all of us as we cycle along.

THE MOUNTAIN BIKE CONTROVERSY

Are Mountain Bikes Environmental Outlaws?
Do We have the Right to Use Public Trails?

We have long endured the animosity of people in the backcountry who complain about a *mountain bike menace*. Many people believe that our fat tires and knobby tread do unacceptable environmental damage, and our uncontrollable riding habits are a danger to animals and other trail users. To the contrary, studies and tests have shown that mountain bikes have no more environmental impact than hiking boots or horse shoes. This does not mean, however, that mountain bikes have zero impact. Wherever man treads, there is an impact. By riding responsibly, though, it is possible to leave only a minimum impact, something we all must take care to achieve.

Unfortunately, it is often people in positions of greatest influence who see mountain bikes as the environment's greatest adversary. Consequently, we as mountain bike riders must be educators, impressing upon everyone that we also deserve the right to use these trails. Our responsibility as bicyclists is no more and no less than any other trail user. We must all take the **soft-cycling** approach, and show that mountain bikes are not environmental outlaws.

ETIQUETTE OF MOUNTAIN BIKING/ SOFT-CYCLING

Moving softly across the land means leaving no more than an echo
Hank Barlow.

When discussing mountain biking etiquette, we are in essence discussing the **soft-cycling** approach. This term, as mentioned before, describes the art of minimum-impact bicycling, and should apply to both the physical and social dimensions of the sport. Make no mistake, however. It is possible to ride fast and furiously while still maintaining the balance of **soft-cycling**. Here are some ways to minimize the impact of mountain bike riding.

- **Do not disturb the soil.** Follow a line within the trail that will not disturb or damage the soil.
- **Avoid trails that, for all but God are considered impassable and impossible.** Don't take a leap of faith down a kamikaze descent where you will be forced to lock your brakes and skid to the bottom, ripping the ground apart as you go.
- **Do not ride over soft or wet trails.** After a rain shower or during the thawing season, trails will often become puddled with mud. Instead of blasting through each section of mud, which may seem both easier and more fun, lift the bike and walk past. Each time a cyclist rides through a soft or muddy section of trail, that part of the trail is permanently damaged.
- **Stay on the trail.** Don't ride around fallen trees that block your path. Stop and cross over them. When you come to a vista overlooking a deep valley, don't ride off the trail for a better vantage point. Instead, leave the bike and walk to see the view. Riding off the trail may seem inconsequential when done just once, but soon someone else will follow, then others, and the cumulative results can be catastrophic. Each time you wander from the trail you begin creating a new path, adding one more scar to the earth's surface.

Soft-cycling should apply to the social dimensions of the sport as well, as mountain bikers are not the only folks who use the trails. Hikers, equestrians, skiers, and other outdoors people use many of the same trails, and can be easily spooked by a marauding mountain biker tearing through the forest.

We should not want to destroy another person's enjoyment of the outdoors. By riding in the backcountry with caution, control, and responsibility, our presence should be felt positively by other trail users. Doing this, trail riding, a privilege that can quickly be taken away, will continue to be ours to share.

RULES OF THE TRAIL

The International Mountain Bicycling Association (IMBA) has developed these guidelines to trail riding. These "Rules of the Trail" are accepted worldwide and will go a long way in keeping trails open. Please respect and follow the "Rules of the Trail" for everyone's sake.

1. **Ride on open trails only.** Respect trail and road closures (if you're not sure, ask a Park or State official first), do not trespass on private property and obtain permits or authorization if required. Federal and State wilderness areas are off-limits to cycling. Parks and state forests may also have certain trails closed to cycling.
2. **Leave no trace.** Be sensitive to the dirt beneath you. Even on open trail you should not ride under conditions where you will leave evidence of your passing, such as on certain soils or shortly after a rainfall. Observe the different types of soils and trails you're riding on, practicing minimum-impact cycling. Never ride off the trail, don't skid your tires, and be sure to pack out at least as much as you pack in.
3. **Control your bicycle!** Inattention for even a second can cause disaster for yourself or for others. Excessive speed frightens and injures people, gives mountain biking a bad name, results in trail closures, and has no excuses.
4. **Always yield.** Let others know you're coming well in advance (a friendly greeting is always good and often appreciated). Startling someone is not considerate or beneficial to the sport. Show your respect when passing others by slowing to walking speed or stopping altogether, especially in the presence of horses. Horses can be unpredictable and cause much pain. Anticipate that other trail users may be around corners or in blind spots.
5. **Never spook animals.** All animals are spooked by a sudden movement, an unannounced approach, or loud noises. Give the animals extra room and time so they can adjust to you. Move slowly or dismount around animals. Running cattle and disturbing wild animals is a serious offence. Leave gates as you find them, or as marked.
6. **Plan ahead.** Know your equipment, your ability, and the area in which you are riding, and plan your trip accordingly. Be self-sufficient at all times, keep your bike in good repair, and carry necessary supplies for changes in weather or other conditions. Keep trails open by setting an example of responsible, courteous, and controlled mountain bike riding for all mountain bikers.
7. **Always wear a helmet when you ride.** For your own safety and protection, a helmet should be worn whenever you are riding your bike. You never know when a tree root or small rock will throw you the wrong way and send you tumbling.

★ According to R.O.M.P., Responsible Organized Mountain Peddlers of Campbell, California, "thousands of miles of dirt trails have been closed to mountain bicycling because of the irresponsible riding habits of just a few riders." Don't follow the example of those few riders. Don't take away trail privileges from thousands of others who work so hard every year to keep the backcountry avenues open to us all.

CYCLING'S NECESSITIES

When discussing the most important things to have on a bike ride, cyclists generally agree upon four things:

- **HELMET**. The reasons to wear a helmet should be obvious. Helmets are discussed in more detail in the *Be Safe, Wear Your Armor* section.
- **WATER**. Without it, cyclists can easily become dehydrated and suffer not only from fatigue, but dizziness, and may collapse. On a warm day, cyclists should drink at least **one full bottle** during **each hour** of riding. It's always good to remember to drink before you feel thirsty. Otherwise, it will be too late.
- **CYCLING SHORTS**. These are necessary if you plan to ride your bike more than twenty to thirty minutes. Padded cycling shorts may be the only thing preventing your derriere from getting serious saddle soreness by ride's end. There are two types of cycling shorts you can buy. Touring shorts are good for people who don't want to look like they're wearing skin-tight cycling shorts. These look like regular shorts, pockets and all, but have built-in padding in the crotch area for protection from chaffing and saddle sores. The more popular, traditional cycling shorts are made of skin-tight lycra material. These also have a padded crotch. Whichever style you find most comfortable, cycling shorts are a necessity for longer rides.
- **FOOD**. This essential item will keep you pedaling. Cycling burns up a lot of calories, and is among the few sports in which bonking occurs. Bonking feels like it sounds. When you bonk your blood sugar level collapses because there is no longer energy in your body. This instantly results in total fatigue and lightheadedness. So, when you're filling your water bottle, remember to bring along some food. You can bring along fruit, an energy bar, or some other form of high energy food. Candy bars are not recommended because they will deliver a sudden burst of high energy and then let you down soon after, causing you to feel worse than before. Energy bars are available at most bike stores and are similar to candy bars, but provide complex carbohydrate energy and high nutrition rather than the fast-burning simple sugars of a candy bar.

BE PREPARED OR DIE

Essential equipment that will keep you from dying alone in the woods.

- **SPARE TUBE**
- **TIRE IRONS**
- **PATCH KIT**
- **PUMP**

See **Appendix A** for instructions on fixing flat tires.

- **MONEY:** Spare change to call home.
- **SPOKE WRENCH**
- **SPARE SPOKES** (that fit your wheel). Tape these to the chain stay.
- **CHAIN TOOL**
- **ALLEN KEYS:** Bring appropriate sizes to fit your bike.
- **COMPASS**
- **FIRST AID KIT**
- **GUIDEBOOK**
- **MATCHES**

★ In case all else fails and you must start a fire to survive, the guidebook will serve as excellent firestarter.

To carry these items, you may need a bike bag. A bag mounting in front of the handlebars provides quick access to your things, whereas a saddle bag fitting underneath the saddle keeps things out of your way. If you'll be carrying lots of equipment, you may want to consider a set of panniers. These are much larger and mount on either side of each wheel. Many cyclists, however, prefer not to use a bag at all. They just slip all they need into their jersey pockets and off they go.

BE SAFE, WEAR YOUR ARMOR

While on the subject of jerseys, it's crucial we discuss the clothing you must wear to be safe, practical, and stylish. Following is a list of items that will both save you from disaster, outfit you comfortably, and most importantly, keep you looking cool.

- **HELMET**. A helmet is an absolute necessity, protecting your head from absolute destruction. It is the only thing that will not disintegrate into a million pieces after a wicked crash on a descent you shouldn't have been on in the first place. It's important to get a helmet with a solid exterior shell to protect your head from sharp or protruding objects. You can also paste stickers of your favorite bicycle manufacturers on these hard-shelled helmets, giving the manufacturers even more free advertising for your dollar.
- **SHORTS**. Let's just say lycra cycling shorts are considered a major safety item if you plan to ride for more than 20 or 30 minutes at a time. As mentioned in the *Cycling Necessities* section, cycling shorts are well regarded as the leading cure-all for chafing and saddle sores. Cycling shorts are best with a padded "chamois" in the crotch area. If you choose to wear

traditional cycling shorts, it is important that they look as if someone spray painted them onto your body.

- **GLOVES**. You may find well-padded cycling gloves invaluable when traveling over rocky trails and gravelly roads for hours on end. Long fingered gloves may also be useful, as branches, trees, assorted hard objects, and, occasionally, small animals will reach out and whack your knuckles. This often causes slightly more pain than you may already be feeling from the crash you just experienced on the last descent.
- **GLASSES**. Not only do sunglasses make you look cool -- extremely important -- they also protect your eyes from invisible branches, creepy bugs, dirt, ultraviolet rays, losing your contacts, and getting caught sneaking glances at the opposite sex who is also wearing skin tight, revealing lycra.
- **SHOES**. Mountain bike shoes should have a stiff sole to help make pedaling easier, as well as good traction when walking your bike up a trail becomes necessary. Virtually any kind of good outdoor hiking footwear will work, but specific mountain bike shoes (especially those with inset cleats) are best. It is important that these shoes look as ugly as possible. Those closest in style to bowling shoes are, of course, the most popular.
- **JERSEY or SHIRT**. Bicycling jerseys are most popular because of their snug fit and back pockets. When purchasing a jersey, look for ones that are loaded with bright, blinding, neon logos and manufacturer's names. These loudly decorated billboards are also good for drawing unnecessary attention to yourself just before taking a mean spill while trying to hop a curb. A cotton T-shirt is a good alternative in warm weather, but when the weather turns cold, cotton becomes a chilling substitute to the jersey. Cotton retains moisture and sweat against your body, which may cause you to get the chills and the ills.

OH, THOSE CHILLY PENNSYLVANIA DAYS

Not every day has perfect weather, especially in Central Pennsylvania. If the weather chooses not to cooperate on the day you've set aside for a bike ride, it's helpful to be prepared.

- **Wear tights or leg warmers**. These are best in weather below 55 degrees. Knees are sensitive and can develop all kinds of problems if they get cold. Some common problems are tendinitis, bursitis, and arthritis.
- **Wear plenty of layers on your upper body**. When the air has a nip in it layers of clothing will help keep the chill away from your chest and prevent the chance of developing bronchitis. If the air is cool, a polypropelene long-sleeved shirt is best to wear against the skin beneath other layers of clothing. Polypropelene, like wool, wicks away moisture from your skin to keep your body dry. Try to avoid wearing cotton or baggy clothing. Cotton, as I mentioned before, holds moisture like a sponge, and baggy clothing will catch a lot of cold wind. Good cold-weather clothing should fit snugly against

your body, but not be restrictive

- **Wool socks for your feet**. Don't pack too many layers under those shoes though, or you may restrict circulation and your feet will get real cold, real fast.
- **Thinsulate or Gortex gloves**. We may all agree there is nothing worse that frozen feet except, of course, frozen hands. A good pair of Thinsulate or Gortex gloves can generally keep your fingers and hands good and warm.

★ All of this clothing can be found at your local bike store, where the staff should be glad to help you fit into the seasons of the year.

TO HAVE OR NOT TO HAVE: (Other Very Useful Items)

Though mountain biking is new to the cycling scene, there is no shortage of things to buy for you and your bike to make riding better, safer, and easier. I have rummaged through the lists of things and separated the gadgets from the good stuff, coming up with what I believe are items not essential, but sure to make mountain bike riding easier and more enjoyable.

- **TIRES**. Buying yourself a good pair of knobby tires is the quickest way to enhance the off-road handling capabilities of your bike. There are many types of mountain bike tires on the market. Some are made exclusively for very rugged off-road terrain. These big-knobbed, soft rubber tires virtually stick to the ground with endless traction, but when ridden on the pavement tend to deteriorate quickly. There are other tires made exclusively for the road. These tires are called "slicks" and have no tread at all. For the average cyclist, though, a good tire that fits right in between these two should do the trick.
- **TOE CLIPS or CLIPLESS PEDALS**. Ride with more power. **Toe clips** attach to your pedals and strap your feet firmly in place, allowing you to exert pressure on the pedals on both the downstroke and the upstroke. They will increase your pedaling efficiency by 30% to 50%. **Clipless pedals**, which liberate your feet from traditional toe clips, have made toe clips virtually obsolete. These act like ski bindings, attaching your shoe directly to the pedal. They are, however, much more expensive than toe clips.
- **BAR ENDS**. These great clamp-on additions to your original straight bar will provide an excellent grip for climbing and a more natural position for your hands.
- **FANNY PACK**. This is great for carrying keys, extra food, guidebooks, tools, a spare tube, and a cellular phone to call for help.
- **SUSPENSION FORKS**. For the more serious off-roaders who want nothing to impede their speed on the trails, investing in a pair of suspension forks can be a good idea. Like tires, there are plenty of brands to choose from and they all do the same thing -- absorb the brutal beating of a rough trail. The cost of these forks, however, is sometimes more brutal than the trail itself.

- **BIKE COMPUTERS**. These are fun gadgets to own, and are no longer very expensive. They have such features as trip distance, speed, odometer, time of day, altitude, alarm, average speed, maximum speed, and the list goes on. Bike computers will come in handy when following these maps.

TYPES OF OFF-ROAD TERRAIN

Before we begin roughing it off road, we may first have to ride the pavement. Please, don't be dismayed. Some of the best rides in the country, I think, are on the road. Once past these smooth-surfaced pathways, however, adventures in dirt await us.

- **FIRE ROADS.** Much of your time will be spent on these scenic back roads winding around the mountains. These dirt and gravel roads are used primarily as access to forest land and are kept in good condition.
- **SINGLETRACK**. Singletrack can be the most fun on a mountain bike. These trails are often very narrow, steep, and technical, and you will never encounter any automobiles. It is important to make sure it's legal to ride on each trail before attacking these rugged pathways. (All trails and roads in this guidebook are open to mountain bikes.) It is also very important to control your speed on these trailways should a hiker or equestrian sharing the same trail appear suddenly from around a hidden turn.
- **OPEN LAND**. Unless there is a marked trail through a field or open land, you should not plan to ride here. Once one person cuts their wheels through a field or meadow, many more are sure to follow, causing irreparable damage to the landscape. A wise person once said, "Human tracks are like cancer cells, they spread very quickly."

TECHNIQUES TO MOUNTAIN BIKE RIDING

Many of us see ourselves as pure athletes; ones with power, strength, and endless endurance. It may be those with the most finesse, balance, agility, and grace, however, that get around most quickly on a mountain bike. Although power, strength, and endurance have their place in mountain biking, the emphasis when riding does not necessarily fall on them with as much importance as it would in other sports.

The bike should become an extension of your body. Slight shifts of your hips or knees can have remarkable results. Experienced bike handlers will seem to flash down technical descents, dashing over obstacles in a smooth and graceful effort as though floating above the earth.

Here are some tips and techniques to help you zip up and around the hills and valleys without touching the ground or breaking a sweat.

Braking

Using your brakes requires you to use your head, especially when descending. This doesn't mean using your head as a stopping block, but rather to think, using your best judgment about how much or how little to squeeze those brake levers.

The more weight a tire is carrying, the more braking power it has. When you're going downhill, your front wheel carries more weight than the rear. Braking then with the front brake will help keep you in control without going into a skid. Be careful, though, not to overdo it with the front brakes and toss yourself over the handlebars, and don't neglect your rear brake. When descending, shift your weight back over the rear wheel, thus increasing your rear braking power as well. This will balance the power of both brakes and give you the most control.

Good riders learn how much to shift their weight over each wheel, and to apply just enough braking power to each brake, being careful not to "endo" over the handlebars or skid down a trail.

GOING UPHILL: Climbing Those Treacherous Climbs

- **Shift into a low gear**. (Push the thumb shifter away from you). Before shifting, be sure to ease up on your pedaling before each shift so there is not too much pressure on the chain. Find the gear that's best for you to match the terrain and steepness of each climb.
- **Stay seated**. Standing out of the saddle is often helpful when climbing steep hills on a road bike, but you may find that on a mountain bike, standing can cause your rear tire to loose traction and spin out from under you. You're on loose dirt now rather than on pavement. Staying seated will keep your weight over the rear wheel, giving the tire better traction. Climbing may prove to be much easier in the saddle.
- **Lean forward**. On very steep hills, the front wheel may begin to feel unweighted and pop up. Lean forward to compensate by adding more weight over the front wheel.
- **Administer power to those pedals**. Up steep and very technical ascents, keep the pressure and the power pumping into those pedals. This is the only way to keep the bike moving forward. The slower you go through rough trail sections, the harder it is.

GOING DOWNHILL: The Real Reason We Get Up in the Morning

- **Shift into the big chainring.** Shifting into the big ring before a wicked descent will help keep the chain from bouncing off. Should you crash or disengage your leg from the pedal, the chainring teeth of the big ring won't bite into your leg.
- **Relax**. With a death grip on the bars, locked elbows, and tight arms, things can become quite difficult, especially when descending. Bend your elbows, keep a firm but relaxed grip on the handlebars, cover your brakes, and steer with your body. Let your shoulders guide you through each turn and around each obstacle.
- **Don't oversteer and don't lose control.** Mountain biking is much like downhill skiing, as you must shift your weight from side to side down narrow, bumpy descents. Your bike will have the tendency to track in the

direction you look and follow the slight shifts and leans of your body. You should not think so much about steering, but rather in what direction you wish to go.

- **Rise above the saddle**. When racing down bumpy, technical descents, you should not be sitting on your saddle, but standing on your pedals, allowing your legs and knees to absorb the shock of the trail instead of your rear.
- **Drop your saddle**. For very steep, technical descents you may want to drop your saddle three or four inches. This lowers your center of gravity, giving you more room to bounce around.
- **Keep your pedals parallel to the ground**. The front pedal should be slightly higher so as not to catch on small rocks and logs.
- **Stay focused**. Concentrate and stay focused while descending. Many descents require your utmost concentration just to reach the bottom. There may be sense of meditation as you fly down trails. You will become completely absorbed in every groove, every root, every rock, and every hole. If your thoughts wander, so may your bike, and into those trees you will go.

WATCH OUT!

Back-road Obstacles

- **Logs**. These are fun to jump or hop. Be careful to practice on small logs at slow speeds first before you get too confident. It's easy to pull the front wheel up a bit too soon and plant yourself right into the log.
- **Rocks**. They will toss you up and down and all around. Stay relaxed, let your elbows and knees absorb the shock, and always continue to apply power to your pedals. The slower you go, the more time your tires will have to get caught between a rock and a hard place.
- **Water**. Before crossing a stream or puddle, be sure to first check the depth and bottom surface. There may be an unseen canyon or large boulder hidden under the water that will have you all washed up if you're not careful. After you're sure all is safe, hit the water at a good speed and allow the bike to steer you through.
- **Leaves**. Be careful of leaves, especially wet leaves. These may look pretty, but a trail covered with leaves represents an opportunity for your wheels to slip out from under you. Leaves are not nearly as unpredictable and dangerous as ice, but they do warrant your attention on a rainy day.
- **Mud**. It can be a nuisance to some and lots of fun for others. Try not to ride through muddy sections of trail. If possible, walk your bike around the muddy sections to avoid causing permanent damage to trails. Also, be sure to clean any mud off your bikes when you get home. Neglecting your bike may lead to all sorts of mechanical problems.

Urban Obstacles

- **Curbs** are fun to jump, but like logs, be careful. They can also be painful.
- **Drains** usually pose no problems, but be careful not to get a wheel caught in the grate.
- **Dogs** are great pets, but for some reason have it in for bicyclists. Beware of dogs. If you think you can't outrun a dog that's chasing you, stop and walk your bike out of its territory. A loud yell to *Get!* or *Go home!* often works, as does a sharp squirt from your water bottle right between its eyes.
- **Cars** are tremendously convenient when we're in them, but dodging cars on the road can be a major source of inconvenience on the bike. As a cyclist, you must realize most drivers aren't expecting bicyclists to be on *their* road and many drivers would prefer that cyclists stay off the roads altogether. So be cautious and careful and always clearly signal all of your intentions.
- **Potholes**. Like grates and back-road canyons, potholes should be avoided. Just because you're on an all-terrain bicycle doesn't mean that you're indestructible. Potholes can damage rims, pop tires, and sometimes even throw you off the bike. For outdoor bicycle air acrobatics, potholes are great, but should otherwise be strictly avoided.

LAST MINUTE CHECKOVER

Before a ride, it's a good idea to give your bike a once-over to make sure everything is in working order. Begin by checking the air pressure in your tires before each ride to make sure they are properly inflated. Mountain bikes require about 45 to 55 pounds per square inch of air pressure. If your tires are underinflated there is greater likelihood that the tubes may get pinched on a bump or rock, causing the tire to flat.

Looking over your bike to make sure everything is secure and in its place is the next step. Go through the following checklist before each ride. It probably will take you less than a minute to complete unless, of course, your bike is falling apart.

- **Pinch the tires to feel for proper inflation.** They should give just a little on the sides, but feel very hard on the treads. If you have a pressure gauge, use that.
- **Check your brakes**. Squeeze the rear brake and roll your bike forward. The rear tire should skid. Next, squeeze the front brake and roll your bike forward. The rear wheel should lift into the air. If this doesn't happen, then your brakes are too loose. Make sure the brake levers don't touch the handlebars when squeezed with full force.
- **Check all quick releases on your bike**. Make sure they are all securely tightened.
- **Lube up**. If your chain squeaks, apply some lubricant.
- **Check your nuts and bolts**. Check the handlebars, saddle, cranks, and

pedals, making sure that each is tight and securely fastened to your bike.

- **Check your wheels**. Spin each wheel, checking to see that they spin through the frame and between brake pads freely.
- **Have you got everything?** Make sure you have your spare tube, tire irons patch kit, frame pump, tools, food, water, and guidebook.

Liability Disclaimer

Beachway Press assumes no liability for cyclists traveling along any of the suggested routes in this publication. The routes shown on the following maps were chosen as introductions to the roads and trailways of the backcountry for their safety, aesthetics, and pleasure, and are deemed acceptable and accommodating to bicyclists. Safety upon these routes, however, cannot be guaranteed. Cyclists must assume their own responsibility when riding these routes and understand that with an activity such as bicycling, there may be unforeseen risks and dangers.

Central Pennsylvania

It was, perhaps, the Susquehannock Indians who first explored Central Pennsylvania's nearly 732,000 acres of state forest land. Lead by the great Indian chief Bald Eagle and the beautiful princess Nita-nee, the Susquehannocks bombed through streams, over logs, around trees, and through mud on bicycles made from dug-out logs long before European colonists ever arrived.

Captain James Potter was the first European to explore the area, pioneering the way for early European settlers and telling stories of his Tour de France glory days. These people found the area rich in limestone, iron ore, timber, water, and Shimano DEORE XT components.

In 1800, Bellefonte, the center of the state's early iron industry became the County Seat of the newly created Centre County. Shortly after the town's settlement, the influential French statesman Talleyrand visited and hailed the area's Big Spring as "La Bella Fonte!" thereby naming the town.

Throughout the mid to latter half of the 1800s, Central Pennsylvania flourished with a prosperous iron industry that brought with it an explosion in the area's population. The people would soon discover one of the greatest mountain biking regions in the country.

In 1855, seeing the need to accommodate the growing populations and the increasing number of Indians and European settlers racing around in dug-out bicycles, the Pennsylvania Agriculture Society toyed with the idea of building a velodrome and hosting the Grundig World Mountain Bike Championships. Instead, and much to the dismay of the cyclists in the region, they built Farmer's High School, which would later become Pennsylvania State University.

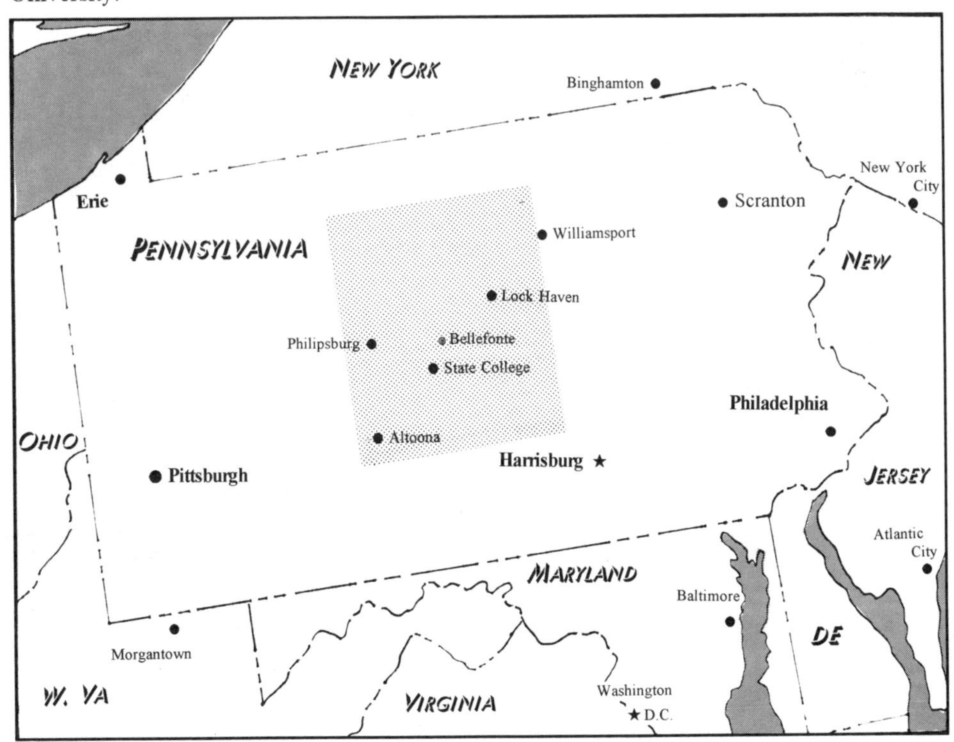

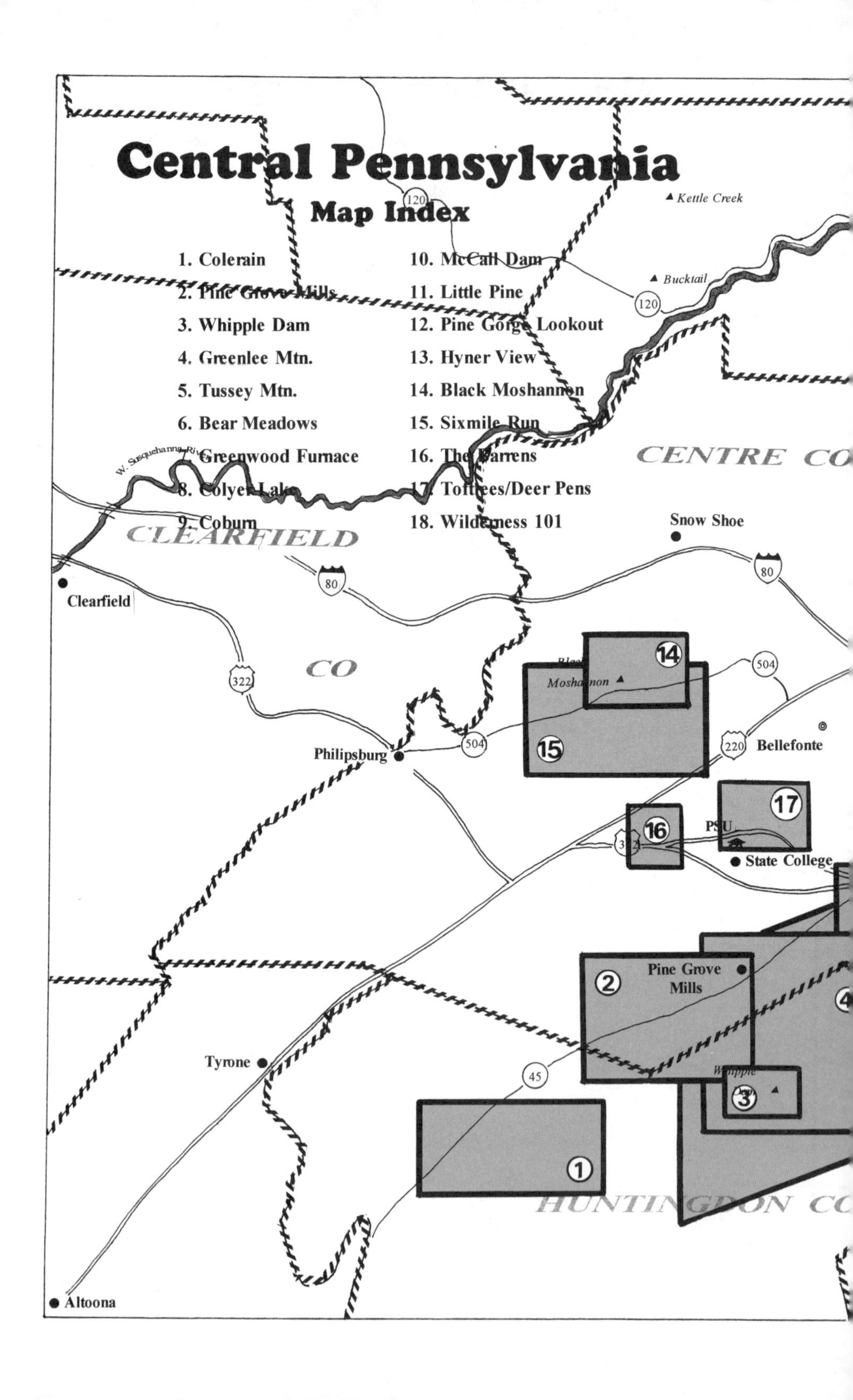
Central Pennsylvania
Map Index
1. Colerain
2. Pine Grove Mills
3. Whipple Dam
4. Greenlee Mtn.
5. Tussey Mtn.
6. Bear Meadows
7. Greenwood Furnace
8. Colyer Lake
9. Coburn
10. McCall Dam
11. Little Pine
12. Pine Gorge Lookout
13. Hyner View
14. Black Moshannon
15. Sixmile Run
16. The Barrens
17. Toftrees/Deer Pens
18. Wilderness 101
Kettle Creek
Bucktail
CENTRE CO
CLEARFIELD CO
HUNTINGDON CO
Snow Shoe
Clearfield
Philipsburg
Bellefonte
PSU
State College
Pine Grove Mills
Tyrone
Altoona
W. Susquehanna River

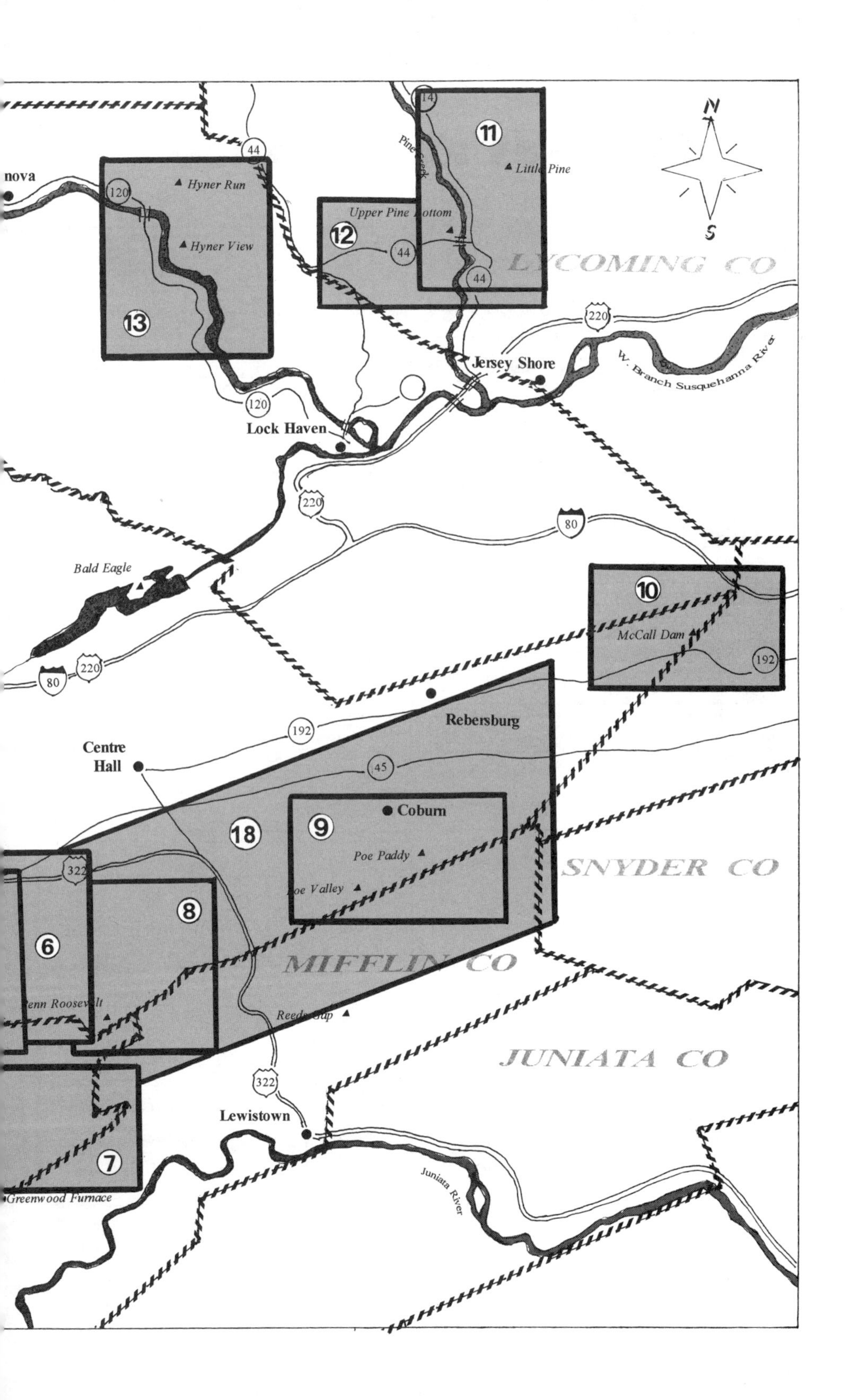
N
S
nova
Hyner Run
Hyner View
Upper Pine Bottom
Little Pine
Pine Creek
LYCOMING CO
Jersey Shore
W. Branch Susquehanna River
Lock Haven
Bald Eagle
McCall Dam
Rebersburg
Centre Hall
Coburn
Poe Paddy
Poe Valley
SNYDER CO
MIFFLIN CO
Reeds Gap
JUNIATA CO
Lewistown
Juniata River
Greenwood Furnace
13
12
11
10
9
18
8
6
7

Courses at a Glance

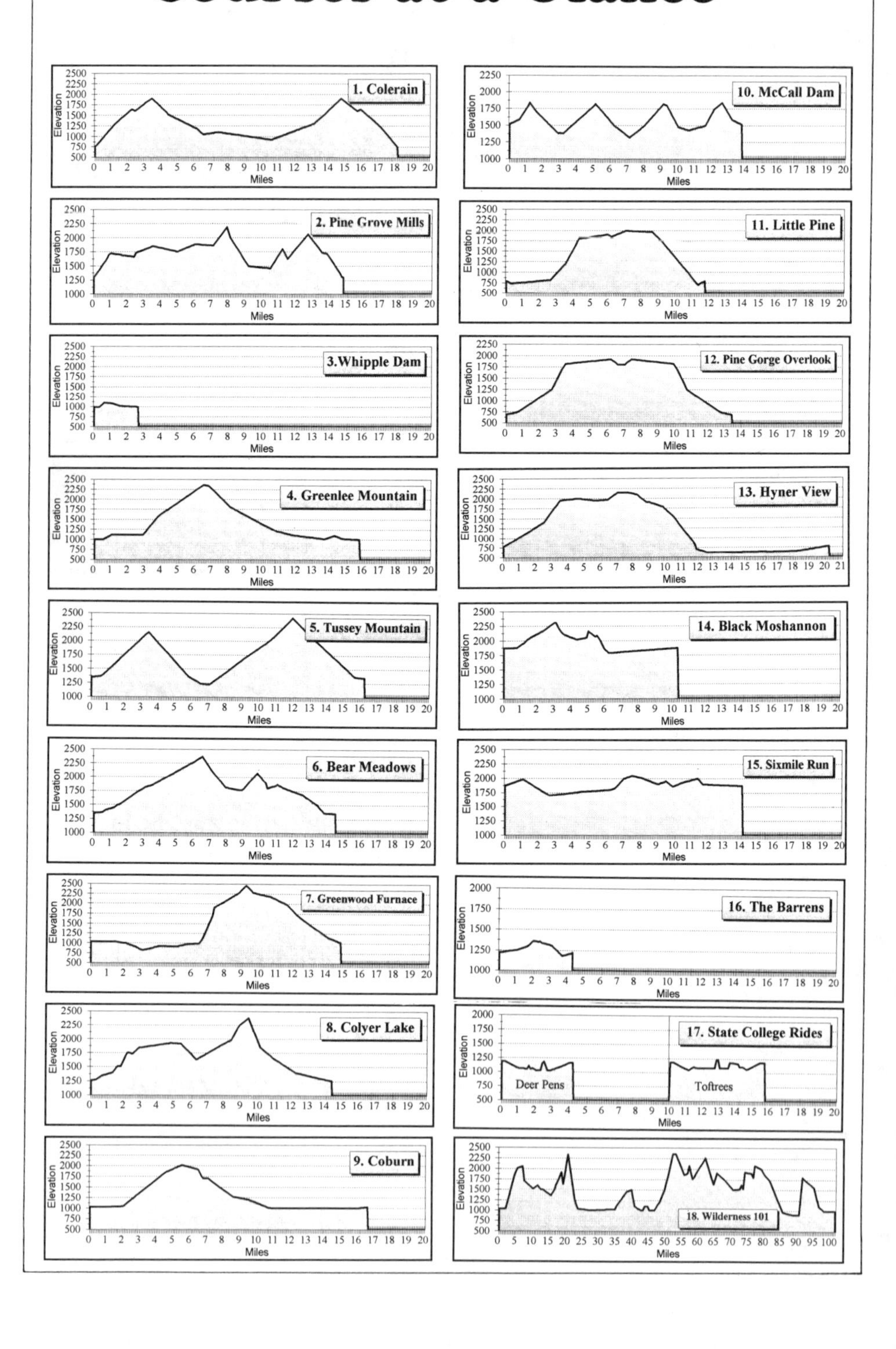

Things To Look For
(Trees, Plants, and Animals)

Central Pennsylvania's state forests are relatively homogenous with regard to species of foliage and wildlife. Here are some of the common trees, plants, and animals you can expect to see while out riding in the backcountry.

Eastern Hemlock. The official State Tree of the Commonwealth of Pennsylvania. This large, long-living tree is found just about anywhere is Pennsylvania's forests. Distinguishable by its dark hue and feathery, irregular branches.

Eastern White Pine. A tree of great commercial importance, the White Pine's soft, light wood probably has more uses than that of any other species. Distinguishable by its tall, straight, dark trunk and horizontally spreading limbs.

White Oak. Wood from the White Oak is used extensively for liquid containers, including whiskey barrels. This tree is broader than it is tall, having a short trunk with light-gray to white bark. It's leaves turn to violet-purple in autumn.

Red Maple. This showy, ornamental tree has a short trunk and a broad, oval head. Distinguishable by its dark, scaly bark, reddish flowers and fruit in the spring, and crimson leaves in autumn.

Gray Birch. This dull white, twiggy tree can be found springing up rapidly in barren soil such as abandoned farmland and fields. Distinguishable by their thin trunks, usually covered by triangular-shaped black patches. Leaves turn a fiery yellow in autumn.

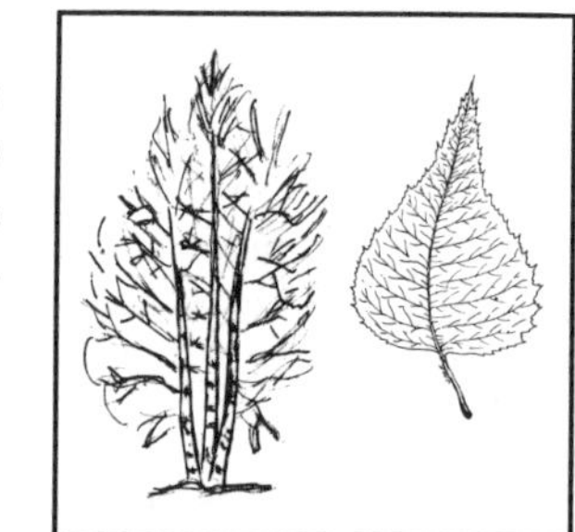

Bitternut Hickory. Preferring wet soils, this tall tree (up to 60 feet) is usually found growing near streams. The hickory nuts are edible, but slightly bitter. In autumn the leaves turn beautiful yellow.

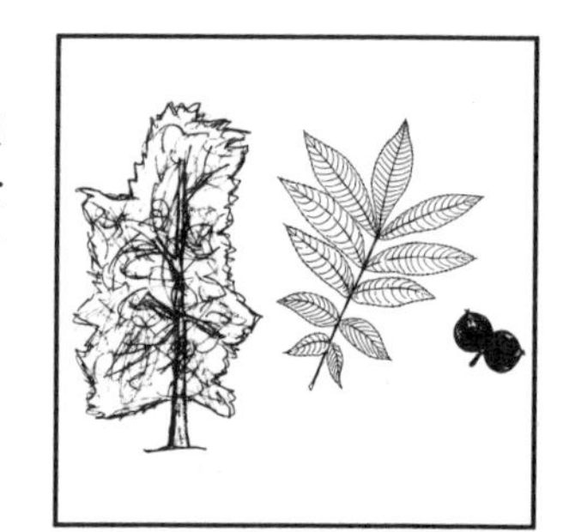

Mountain Ash. You will usually find this small tree growing in the mountains and along hillsides. The thin-trunked Mountain Ash has a smooth, pale-gray bark, producing small, white clusters of flowers that develop into bunches of bright red or orange berries. It's leaves turn clear yellow in autumn.

Mountain Laurel. The official Pennsylvania State Flower. This shrub, which can grow up to 10 feet in height, covers the Pennsylvania mountains and hillsides. Its lacey pink and white blossoms are in bloom well into June.

Huckleberry. This low shrub is found growing sporadically throughout the region. Its white or pink flower clusters develop into the edible huckleberries, which are similar to the closely related blueberries.

Hayscented Fern. These graceful green ferns are found growing in large colonies, carpeting large areas of forest land. Ferns don't flower, but reproduce by spores, usually found on the underside of the leaves. The hayscented fern distributes its spores between July and October.

★ Other trees and plants common to the Central Region that you may see while riding:

- Tulip Poplar (Tuliptree)
- Black Gum
- Rhododendron
- Teaberry
- Prince's Pine

The Animals of the Jungle

Some common species of wildlife you may happen to run into while out pedaling in the woods. If an animal wanders onto your road or path, approach it with caution, giving it extra room and time to adjust to you. Try not to spook an animal. Animals can become quite unpredictable when spooked, and may teach you a lesson you won't soon forget.

Gray Squirrel

White Tail Deer

Wild Turkey

Grouse

Porcupine

Black Bear

The Maps

I don't want anyone, by any means, to feel restricted to just these roads and trails that I have mapped. I hope you will have the same adventurous spirit and use these maps as a platform to dive into Central Pennsylvania's backcountry and discover new routes for yourself. One of the best ways to begin this is to simply turn the map upside down and ride the course in reverse. The change in perspective is fantastic and the ride should feel quite different. With this in mind, it will be like getting two distinctly different rides on each map.

For your own purposes, you may wish to copy the directions for the course onto a small sheet to help you while riding, or photocopy the map and cue sheet to take with you. These pages can be folded into a bike bag or stuffed into a jersey pocket. Please remember to slow or even stop when you want to read the map.

The rides in this book are grouped, for the most part, within the different state forests or other common geographical locations. Each section will begin with a brief description of the particular state forest that group of rides will be in.

After a short introduction of each particular ride, there will be a profile map of the ride followed by a cue sheet which will provide detailed directions and information about each ride.

Wrong turn?

How To Use These Maps

Start: *Colerain Picnic Area*	**Total Elevation Gain:** *2250 feet*
Length: *18.1 miles*	**Riding Time:** *2 hours*
Rating: *Moderate to Difficult*	**Calories Burned:** *1200-2000*

Start indicates where the ride will begin and end. All rides travel in a loop, beginning and ending in the same place.

Length gives you the approximate length of each ride in miles.

Rating is based on a combination of the length and terrain of each ride. Below 10 miles and flat is judged to be ***easy***, 10-15 miles is considered ***moderate***, and 15+ miles and hilly is rated ***difficult***.

Total Elevation Gain tells you how many total feet of climbing you did on that particular ride.

Riding Time is an approximate amount of time that particular ride may take. Average speed for a mountain bike is between 10 and 20 miles per hour.

Calories Burned tells you about how many calories are burned during each ride. Bicycling burns between 600-1000 calories per hour of riding.

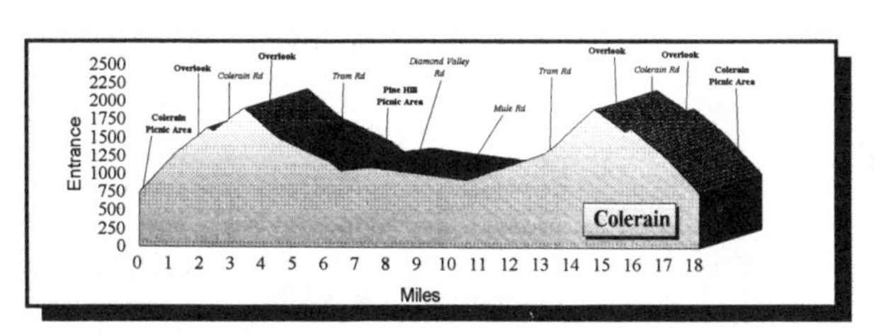

Ride profile. The three-dimensional profile map gives you a cross-sectional look at the ride's ups and downs. The ride's **elevation** is labeled on the left, **mileage** is indicated along the bottom, **points of interest** are shown above the map in **bold face**, and **road** and **trail names**, also above the map, are indicated in *italic*.

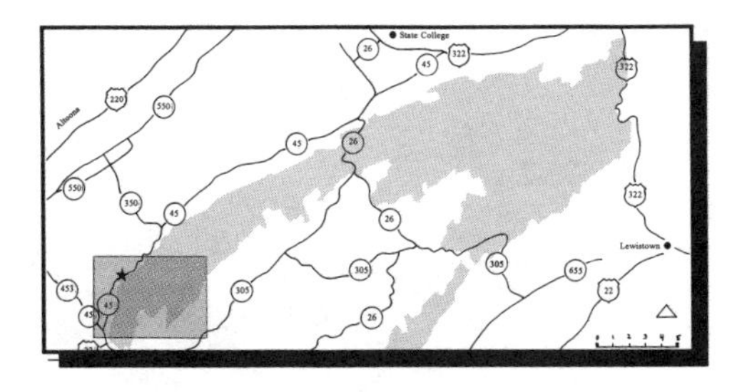

Ride location map. This map shows you where in relation to its particular region the ride is located. The area highlighted is the region on the full-sized trail map.

Rothrock State Forest

The bulk of Rothrock State Forest's nearly 90,000 acres is situated in northern Huntingdon, western Mifflin, and southern Centre Counties. Named in honor of Dr. Joseph Trimble Rothrock, Pennsylvania's Father of Forestry, Rothrock State Forest has an interesting historical background filled with Indians, pioneers, and lots of mountain terrain.

The Delaware Indians, as legend has it, built what is called the "Indian Steps" between Spruce Creek and Stone Creek. These steps made travel over Tussey Mountain much quicker. Jack Mountain is named for the famous Indian fighter, Captain Jack Armstrong. And nearby Bald Eagle and Nittany Mountains, named after the great Susquehannock Indian chief Bald Eagle and princess Nita-nee and Indian Caverns near Colerain add to the Indian lore of Rothrock State Forest.

Rothrock's mountain streams are swollen with trout, and its forest land is alive with wild animals, including grouse, deer, turkey, porcupine, bear, and many other species of small game.

Two state parks are located within the boundaries of Rothrock's main region. Whipple Dam State Park and Greenwood Furnace State Park.

There are five areas designated as State Forest Natural Areas, each possessing beauty, significance, and uniqueness unequalled anywhere else: Alan Seeger Natural Area with its magnificent virgin hemlock and white pine; Detweiler Run, characterized by its virgin white pine, hemlock, and unusually large rhododendron; Bear Meadows, a "botanist's paradise"; Little Juniata with its exposed massive Tuscarora sandstone formation; and Big Flat Laurel, featuring several acres of Pennsylvania's state flower, the Mountain Laurel.

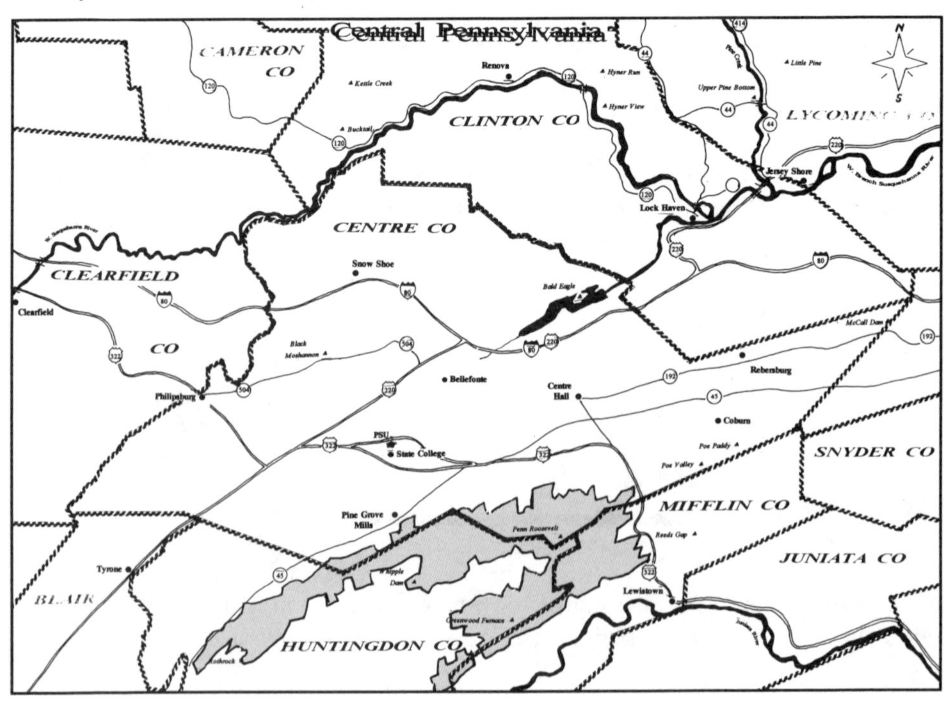

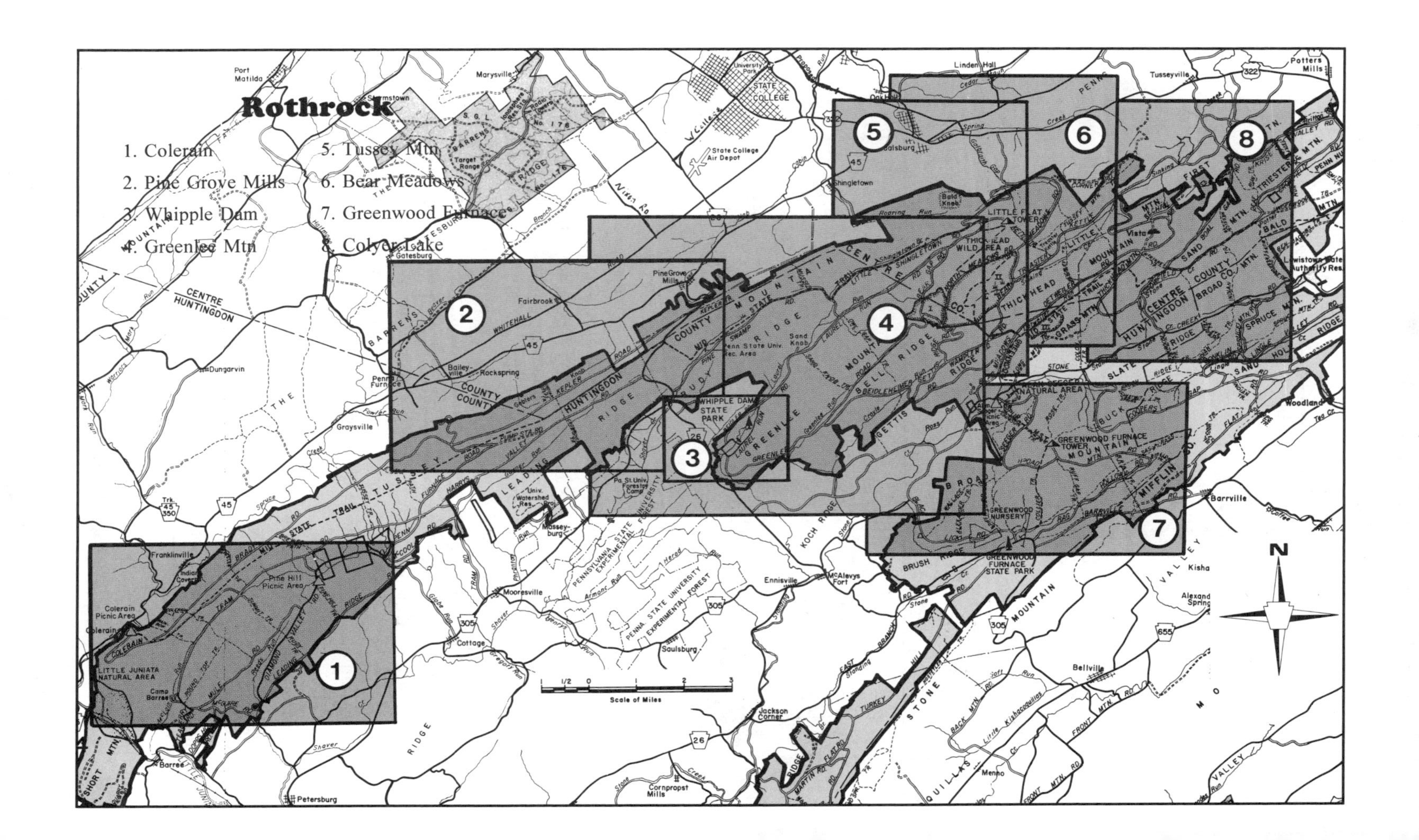
Rothrock
1. Colerain
2. Pine Grove Mills
3. Whipple Dam
4. Greenlee Mtn
5. Tussey Mtn
6. Bear Meadows
7. Greenwood Furnace
8. Colyer Lake
Scale of Miles
N

1. COLERAIN

Start: *Colerain Picnic Area*	**Total Elevation Gain:** *2250 feet*
Length: *18.1 miles*	**Riding Time:** *2-2½ hours*
Rating: *Moderate to Difficult*	**Calories Burned:** *1200-2000*

It's almost like being out west as this ride lassos itself around Round Top Mountain located in old Indian country.

Just up the road from Colerain Picnic Area is Indian Caverns, filled with Indian relics, limestone formations, guided tours, and gift shop. The Little Juniata Natural Area is just south of Colerain, significant for the exposed Tuscarora sandstone formation, measured over 130 feet thick.

This ride, along nearly all unpaved fire roads, takes you over Tussey Mountain, revealing a number of scenic vistas before dropping down the other side to circle the base of Round Top Mountain. The climbs are challenging and the scenery rewarding. Filled with oak, maple, and birch, the fall colors and summer green on this ride are absolutely breathtaking.

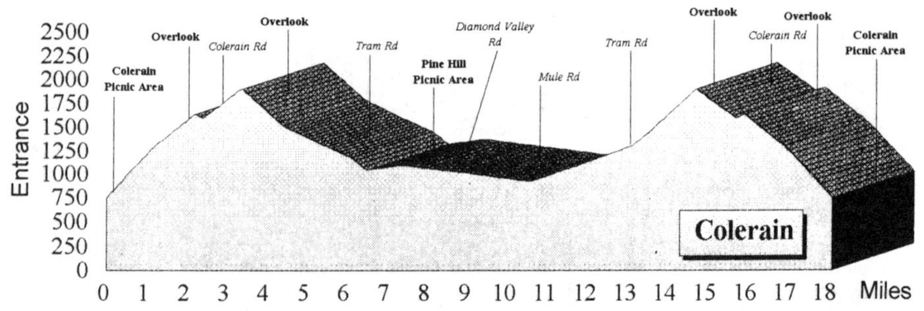

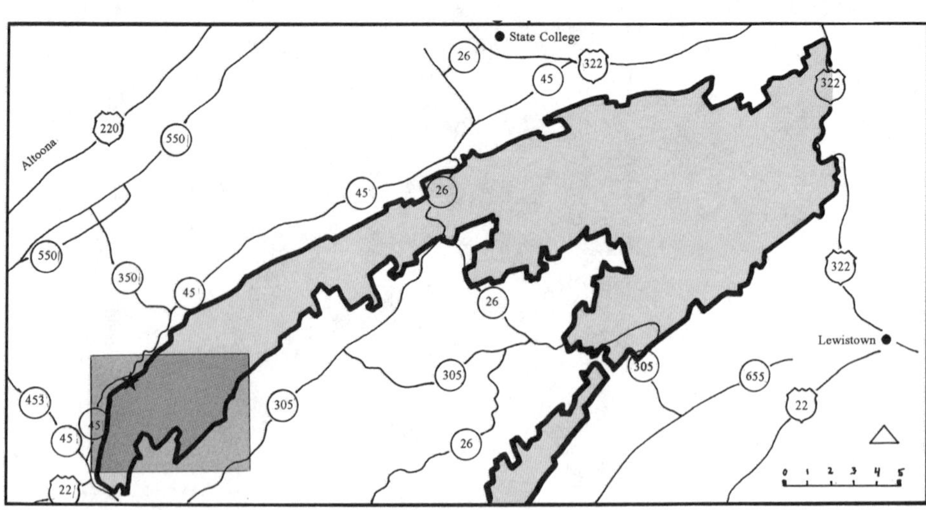

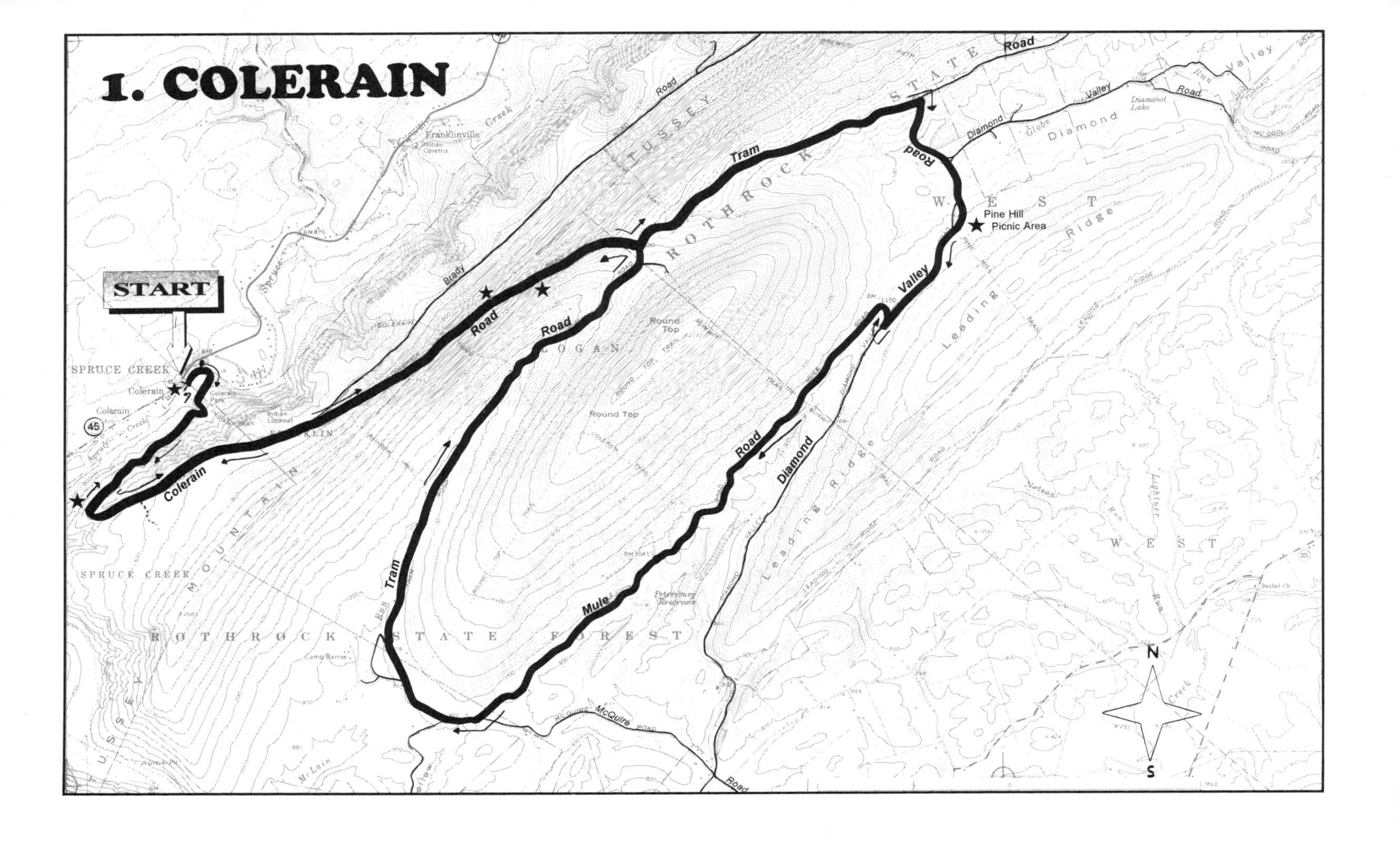
1. COLERAIN
START
Pine Hill
Picnic Area
N
S

Colerain

Where To Begin ☞ *Just off Rte 45 near Spruce Creek, 20 miles west of State College, 20 miles east of Altoona*

MILES	DISTANCE	DIRECTIONS
0.0	0.0	**START** at **Colerain Picnic Area** just off **RTE 45**. Head northeast from the parking lot onto **COLERAIN RD**, which bears right, climbing up Tussey Mtn.
1.2	1.2	★ Scenic vista on the right overlooking the valley.
2.4	1.2	Bear **right** at the fork, past Brady Rd, continuing on **COLERAIN RD**. This climbs to the top.
3.3	0.9	★ Scenic overlook on the left.
3.4	0.1	Reach the summit of Tussey Mtn. Start descending.
3.7	0.3	★ Overlook McLain Run Valley on the right.
4.4	0.7	Reach the bottom of the descent. Turn **left** onto **TRAM RD**.
6.1	1.7	Turn **right** at this intersection onto **DIAMOND VALLEY RD**.
6.4	0.3	Pass a bulldozed area.
6.5	0.1	**DIAMOND VALLEY RD** turns to pavement. Stay **right** toward Pine Hill Picnic Area.
6.6	0.1	Pass **Pine Hill Picnic Area** on the left. Stop and have a sandwich and Power Bar. You're going to have some more climbing to do!
7.4	0.8	Hard **right** off of **DIAMOND VALLEY RD** onto **MULE RD**. This changes back to gravel.
10.6	3.2	Bear **right** at the intersection onto paved road.
10.7	0.1	Bear **right** passed Camp Barree onto **TRAM RD**.

13.1	2.4	Start Climbing. You will soon be heading back over Tussey Mtn and away from Round Top.
13.7	0.6	Turn **left** onto **COLERAIN RD**. Make your way back over the mountain.
14.4	0.7	★ Overlook McLain Run Valley on the left.
14.7	0.3	Reach the summit of Tussey Mtn. Begin the descent.
14.8	0.1	★ Scenic overlook on the right.
15.7	0.9	Bear **left** at the intersection, past Brady Rd, continuing on **COLERAIN RD**.
16.9	1.2	★ Vista overlooking the valley to the left at the hairpin turn.
18.1	1.2	Reach the bottom and you're back at **Colerain Picnic Area**, where it's time to set up the picnic basket and pull out the wine.

2. PINE GROVE MILLS

Start: *Pine Grove Mills*	**Total Elevation Gain:** *1800 feet*
Length: *14.6 miles*	**Riding Time:** *1-1½ hours*
Rating: *Moderate to Difficult*	**Calories Burned:** *600-1000*

Paved roads, forest roads, jeep trails, and singletrack: this ride's got some of everything. The ride begins heading straight up Tussey Mountain. You will experience steep wooded trails, rugged singletrack, a short, steep hike, and a leisurely forest road. And all this before reaching the summit and an incredible view of Stone Valley.

Pump Station Road is guaranteed to be a thriller. Just be careful, keep your contacts in your eyes, and don't go over the edge!

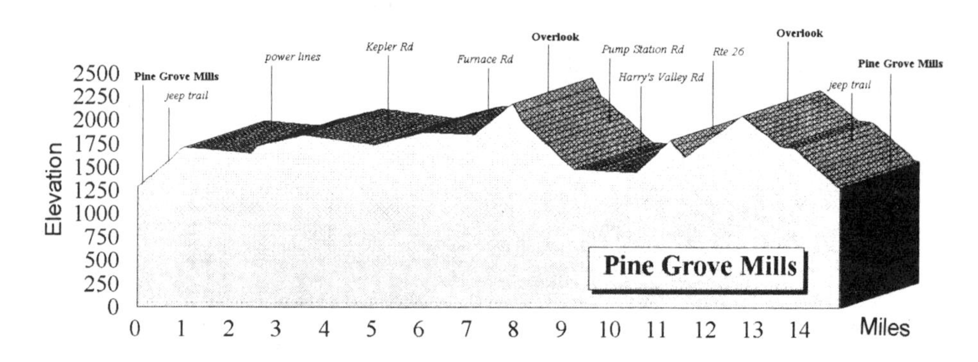

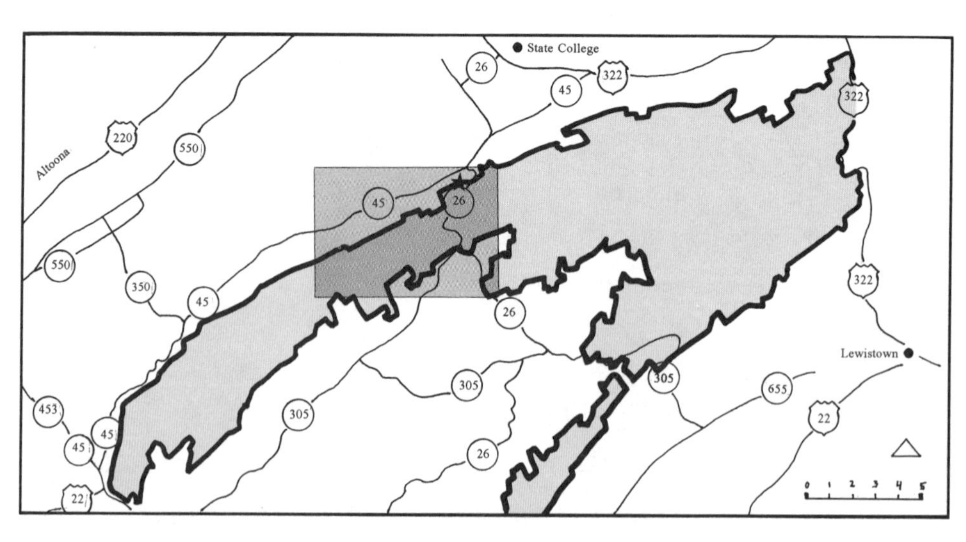

2. PINE GROVE MILLS

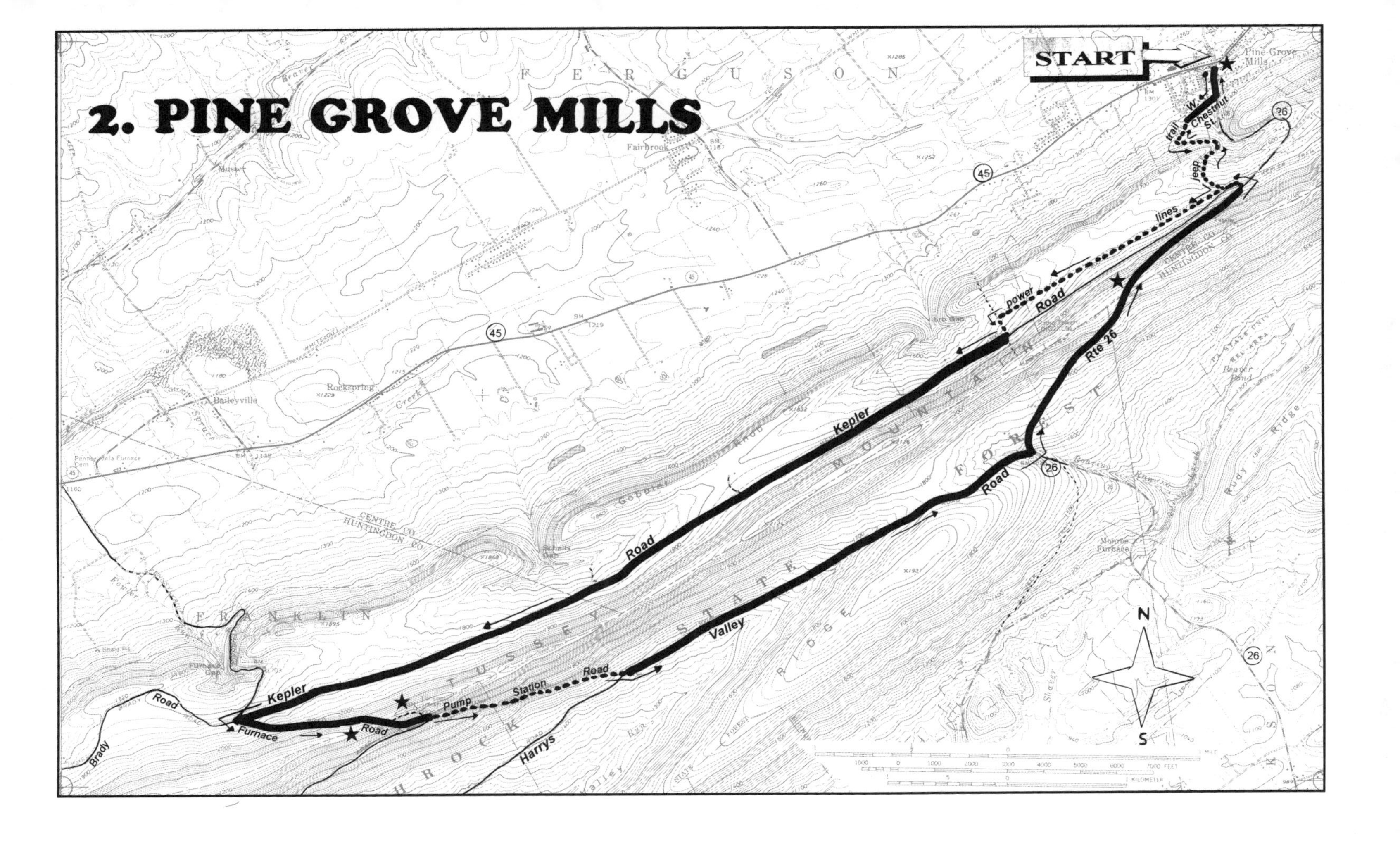

Pine Grove Mills

Where To Begin ☞ *The corner of Rte. 45 and Rte. 26 South, 9 miles south of State College*

MILES	DISTANCE	DIRECTIONS
0.0	0.0	**START** in the small town of **Pine Grove Mills** at the gas station on the corner of **RTE 45 and RTE 26.** Begin climbing up **RTE 26 South**.
0.15	0.15	Turn **right** onto **W. CHESTNUT ST**. Follow this to the steel gate.
0.25	0.1	Go around the **steel gate** and follow the **JEEP TRAIL** into the woods.
0.3	0.05	Take the ***FIRST*** **left** turn onto a narrow singletrack trail heading up the mountain.
0.4	0.1	Bear **left** onto the next narrow trail.
0.5	0.1	This trail take a hard **right** and continues up the mountain.
0.6	0.1	Turn **left** onto a wider **JEEP TRAIL**. This trail heads straight up Tussey Mtn.
0.8	0.2	Come to a small trail intersection. Continue **straight**, heading up the mountain.
1.0	0.2	Reach the summit of Tussey Mtn. Exit out underneath the **POWER LINES**.
1.1	0.1	Turn **right** onto the worn trail that runs beneath the **POWER LINES**.
2.4	1.3	The **power lines** end abruptly, turning perpendicular to the mountain. Turn **left**, following the power lines and climb straight up the mountain to reach **Kepler Rd**. This is a tough section, but short.

2.5	0.1	Turn **right** onto **KEPLER RD**. This is a dirt service road.
7.1	4.6	Come to a **4-way** intersection. Turn **hard left** onto **FURNACE RD**. This road takes you up to the top.
7.9	0.8	Reach the summit of Tussey Mtn. Start your descent.
		★ Overlook into Stone Valley
		★ Turn **left** at the top and climb the rest of the way to the fire tower. What a view.
8.1	0.2	Continue **straight** where **Furnace Rd** hairpins and follow **PUMP STATION RD** into the woods. This fast grassy trail takes you down to **Harry's Valley Rd**.
9.2	1.1	Reach the bottom of the descent. Turn **left** onto **HARRY'S VALLEY RD.**
11.5	2.3	Turn **left** onto **RTE 26 North** and begin the climb back up the mountain. You'll be back in the woods soon.
12.7	1.2	Reach the summit of Tussey Mtn. Begin descending, but keep a sharp eye out for a sudden **left** turn off **Rte 26**. This takes you back under the **power lines**.
		★ Scenic lookout on the left.
13.5	0.8	Turn **left** off of **Rte 26** back to the **POWER LINES**. Be careful of traffic when making this turn.
13.6	0.1	Turn **right** through a hedge of bushes onto a thin trail that takes you across the power lines. This trail takes you back to the **jeep trail** that you came up in the beginning of the ride.
13.7	0.1	Reenter the woods on the **JEEP TRAIL**. Follow this back downhill to **W. Chestnut St**.
13.9	0.2	Go **Straight** where the two jeep trails intersect.

14.1	0.2	Turn **right** off of the main **jeep trail** onto a narrow **SINGLETRACK** trail.
14.2	0.1	Take a **hard left**, continuing down this singletrack.
14.3	0.1	Bear **right** off this trail, continuing downhill.
14.35	0.05	Turn **right** onto the **JEEP TRAIL**.
14.45	0.1	Reach the **steel gate**. Go around this onto **W. CHESTNUT ST**.
14.6	0.15	Turn **left** onto **RTE 26 South** and coast the rest of the way back down into **Pine Grove Mills** where the corner store waits to feed you.

3. WHIPPLE DAM

Start: *Whipple Dam State Park*
Length: *2.7 miles*
Rating: *Easy*
Total Elevation Gain: *120 feet*
Riding Time: *20-30 minutes*
Calories Burned: *300-500*

Originally several hundred yards downstream, the dam was relocated in 1928 to its present location after the Commonwealth of Pennsylvania declared the old dam was irreparable. The dam is named for the Whipple Family, the long-time operators of the sawmill at the old dam. Whipple Dam State Park now contains 244 acres of scenic woodland, including a guarded beach, swimming, boating, fishing, concessions, picnicking, and more.

This ride takes you on a leisurely loop around the lake and through Laurel Run Natural Area, which is specially designed to protect plants, wildflowers, and animal life.

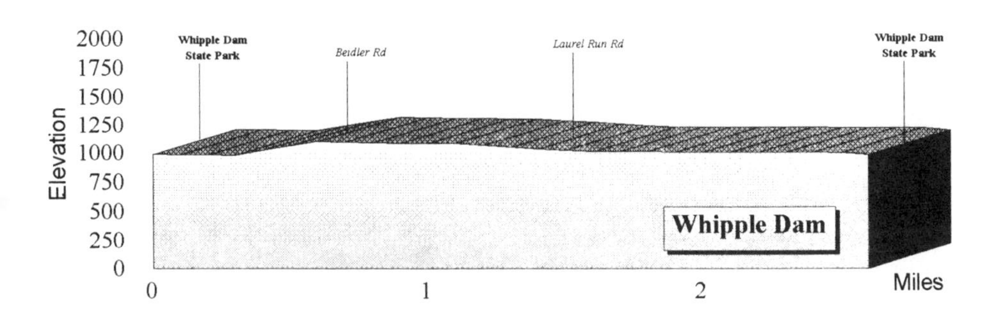

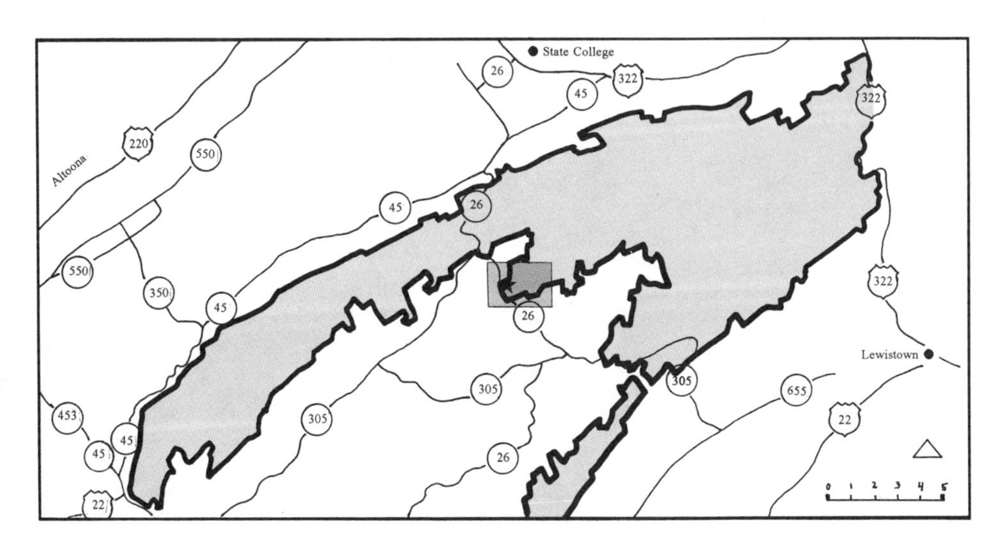

Whipple Dam

Where To Begin ☞ *Whipple Dam State Park, east of Rte. 26, 10 miles south of State College*

MILES	DISTANCE	DIRECTIONS
0.0	0.0	Begin this short ride from Whipple Dam's main parking-visitor area and head west on **BEACH RD** as if exiting the park.
0.1	0.1	Turn **right** onto **WHIPPLE RD**, heading toward the Northwest Shore. **Cross** the bridge over the water falls. This section is all paved.
0.2	0.1	Turn **left** toward the park's exit, continuing on **WHIPPLE RD**.
0.4	0.2	Turn **right** onto **BEIDLER RD** immediately past the wooden median. This dirt road is an up and down adventure through a tunnel of pines, ferns and forest.
		★ **Laurel Run Natural Area** is all of the forest on the right.
1.7	1.3	Turn **right** onto **LAUREL RUN RD** just after the green and white lodge on the left. Beidler Rd ends here, just past a green and white lodge house. Laurel Run Rd becomes paved.
2.6	0.9	Turn **right** at the **Whipple Dam State Park** sign, coasting downhill to the lake.
2.7	0.1	Turn **right** onto **BEACH RD** and head over to the beach for some rest.

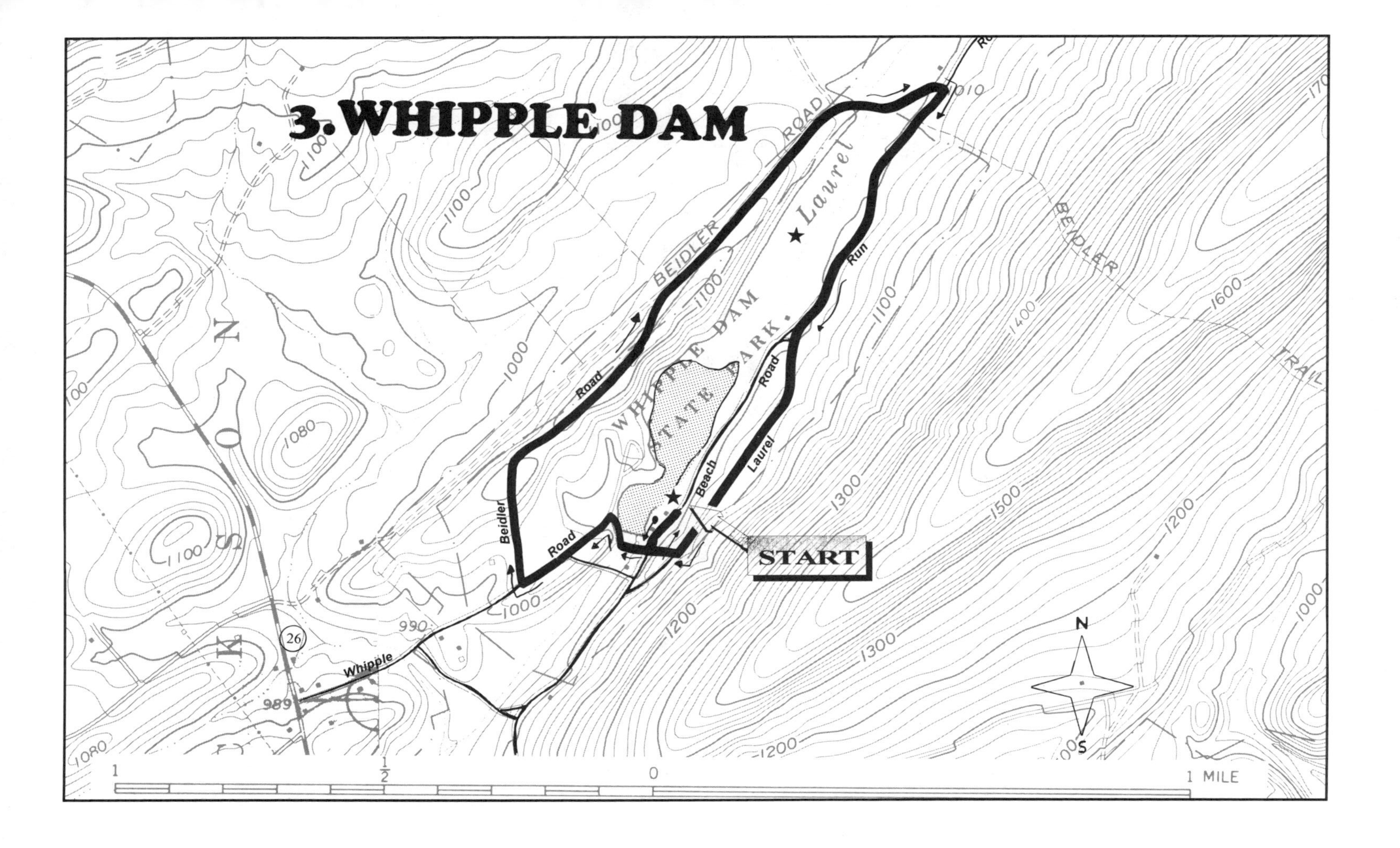
3. WHIPPLE DAM
START
Laurel
Run
BEIDLER
ROAD
TRAIL
WHIPPLE DAM
STATE PARK
Road
Beach
Laurel
Beidler
Road
Whipple
26
989
N
S
1
1/2
0
1 MILE

4. GREENLEE MOUNTAIN

Start: *Whipple Dam State Park*	**Total Elevation Gain:** *1456 feet*
Length: *15.8 miles*	**Riding Time:** *1-2 hours*
Rating: *Moderate*	**Calories Burned:** *1000-2000*

This is a great ride for those of you looking for a real adventure while at Whipple Dam State Park. Like the much shorter ride around Whipple Dam, this ride begins at the beach. However, it then leads you deep into the forest and high atop a mountain plateau where several acres of Mountain Laurel grow thick and beautiful in the Big Flat Laurel Viewing Area. The bloom is fantastic from late May well into June.

The ride circles around Greenlee Mountain, then heads back down to Whipple Dam on a fun descent that is not too technical or demanding. This is a great ride for any level.

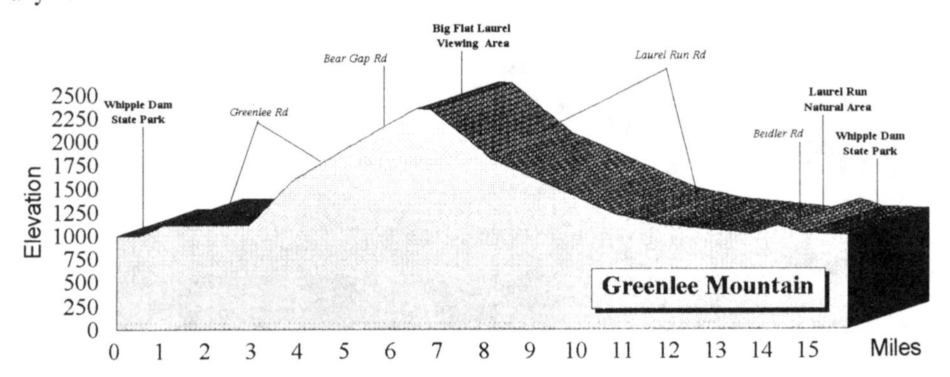

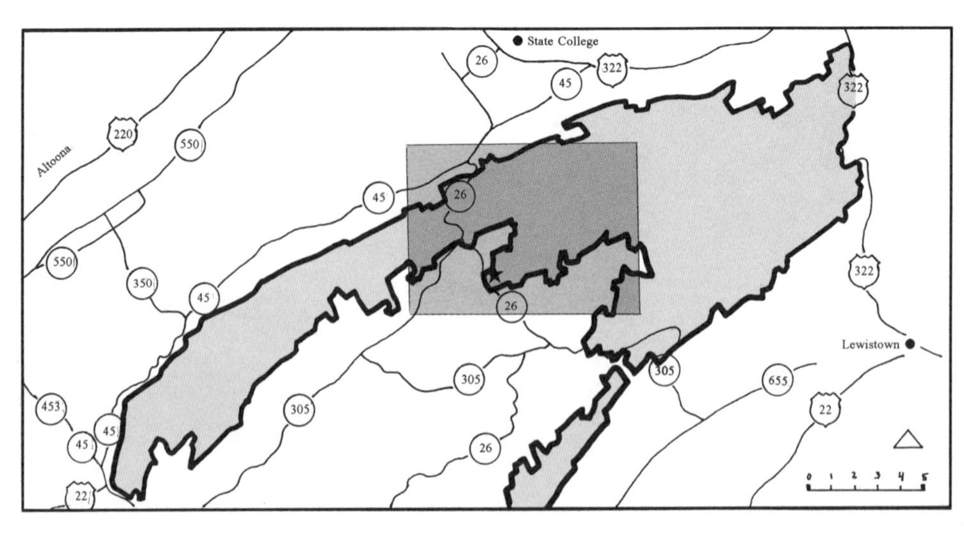

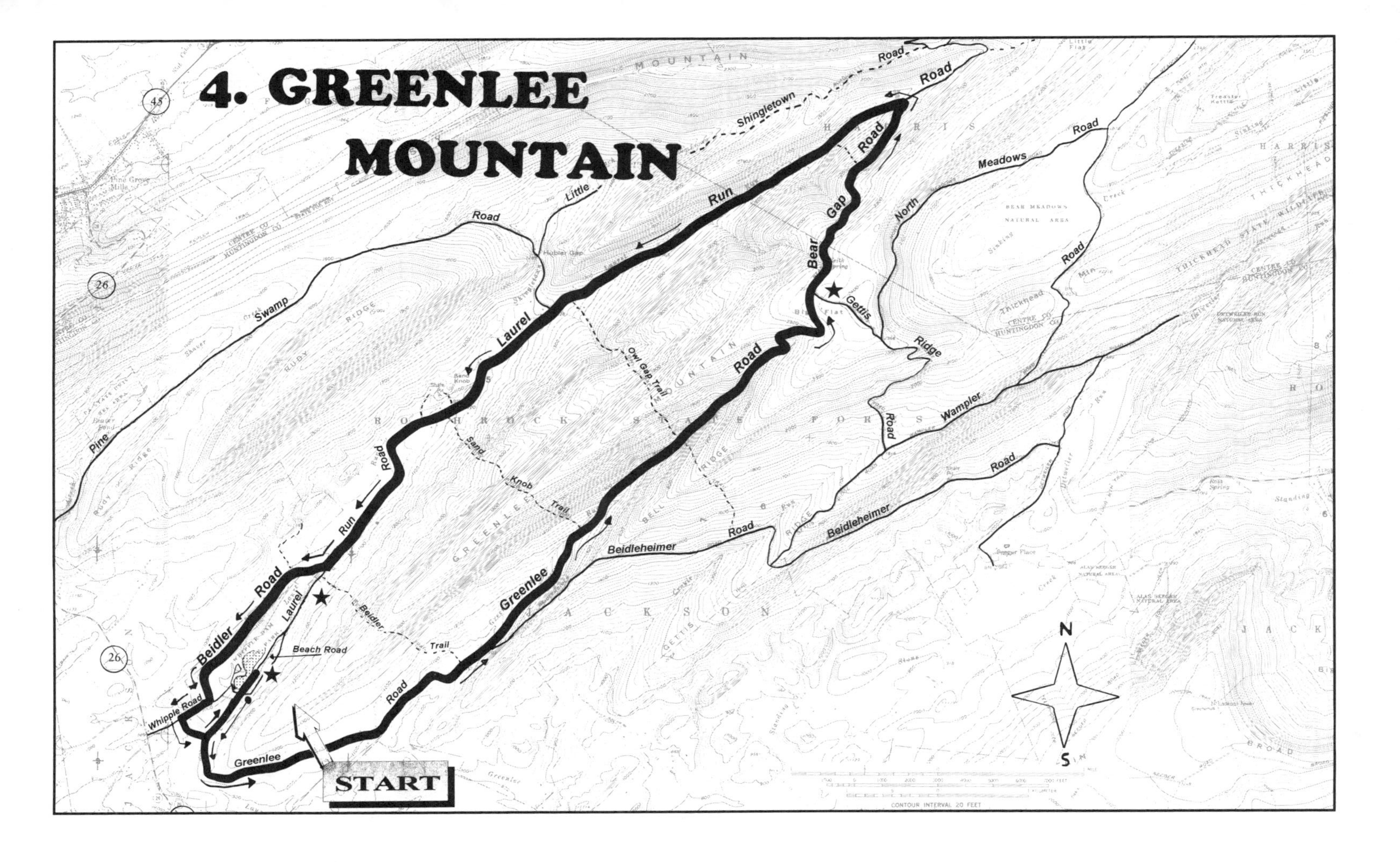

4. GREENLEE MOUNTAIN
START
Greenlee Road
Beidleheimer Road
Bear Gap Road
Gettis Ridge
North Meadows Road
Wampler Road
Laurel Run Road
Beidler Road
Beidler Trail
Whipple Road
Beach Road
Sand Knob Trail
Owl Gap Trail
Shingletown Road
Little Road
Pine Swamp
N
S
CONTOUR INTERVAL 20 FEET

Greenlee Mountain

Where To Begin ☞ *Whipple Dam State Park, east of Rte. 26, 10 miles south of State College*

MILES	DISTANCE	DIRECTIONS
0.0	0.0	**START** at **Whipple Dam State Park's visiting area.** Head west on **BEACH ROAD**.
0.1	0.1	Go **straight**, crossing **WHIPPLE RD** and ride across the large **dirt road** connecting **LAUREL RUN RD**.
0.2	0.1	Go around the wooden gate and turn **right** onto **LAUREL RUN RD**. This road is paved.
0.5	0.3	Turn **left** off of pavement onto **GREENLEE RD**.
1.0	0.5	Reach the top of this first small climb.
2.9	1.9	Bear **left** at the fork, continuing on **GREENLEE RD** toward **Big Flat Laurel Viewing Area**.
3.9	1.0	Begin the climb toward **Big Flat**.
6.5	2.6	Pass **GETTIS RIDGE RD** on the right. Bear **left** onto **BEAR GAP RD**.
		Reach the summit.
6.8	0.3	★ **Big Flat Laurel Viewing Area** near this intersection.
8.1	1.3	Reach the bottom of the descent. Turn **left** onto **LAUREL RUN RD**.
10.2	2.1	Pass Bard Trail on the left.
10.6	0.4	Pass Owl Gap Lodge on the left.
10.8	0.2	Continue **straight** at the intersection with **Pine Swamp Rd,** continuing down **LAUREL RUN RD.**
11.8	1.0	Pass Sand Knob on the right.

13.7	1.9	Turn **right** onto **BEIDLER RD**. You will immediately pass a green and white lodge house on the right. This road is lined with beautiful white pines. ★ Laurel Run Natural Area.
14.8	1.1	Come to a **Stop Sign**. Turn **right** onto **WHIPPLE ROAD**.
15.1	0.3	Turn **left** at the bottom of this little hill. Follow the signs that read "**All Park Traffic**."
15.8	0.7	Arrive back at **Whipple Dam** and go for a swim to cool off.

5. TUSSEY MOUNTAIN

Start: *Tussey Mountain Ski Area*	**Total Elevation Gain:** *1994 feet*
Length: *16 miles*	**Riding Time:** *1-2 hours*
Rating: *Moderate to Difficult*	**Calories Burned:** *1000-1500*

This ride may seem more like a downhill ski run than a bike ride, and what better place to start than Tussey Mountain Ski Area.

Once you've climbed Tussey Mountain, the speed does proceed. The descent down Little Shingletown Road is fast, furious, fantastic, and fun! Watch for plenty of obstacles and plenty of speed.

After climbing back to the top again, take a turn up to the fire tower and catch an incredible view of Rothrock State Forest and Happy Valley to the north. These descents are never long enough, are they?

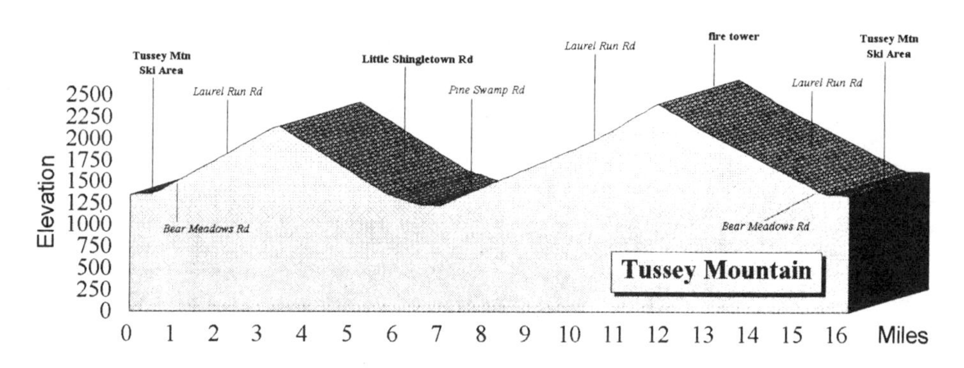

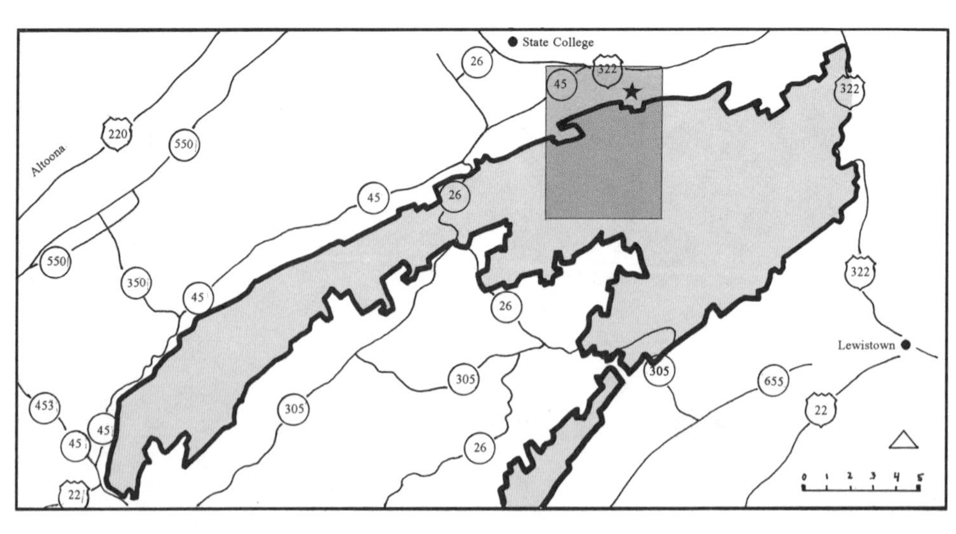

5. TUSSEY MOUNTAIN

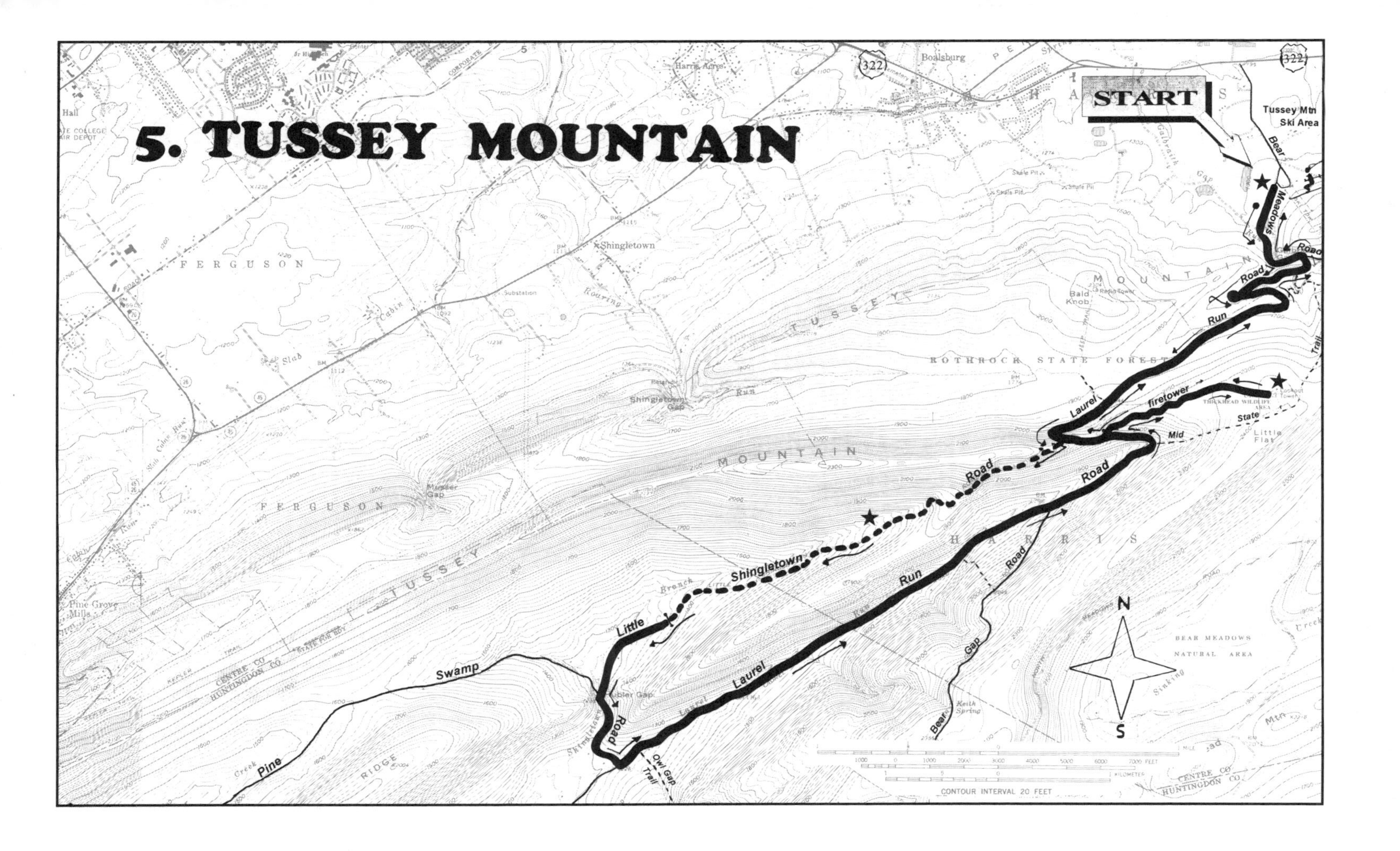

Tussey Mountain

Where To Begin ☞ *Tussey Mtn Ski Area, just off Rte. 322, 6 miles east of State College*

MILES	DISTANCE	DIRECTIONS
0.0	0.0	From the base of **Tussey Mtn.** start pedaling your way into the forest along **BEAR MEADOWS RD.**
0.1	0.1	The pavement on **BEAR MEADOWS RD** deteriorates into a pothole-filled, dirt/asphalt road.
0.3	0.2	**Cross** the first **one-lane bridge**.
0.5	0.2	**Cross** the second **one-lane bridge**. Begin climbing up Tussey Mountain.
0.7	0.2	Turn **right** onto **LAUREL RUN RD**. This gravel service road winds right up to the top. Believe me, though, the raging descent down the other side makes this climb well worth it!
3.2	2.5	Reach the top of the climb! Turn **right** onto **LITTLE SHINGLETOWN RD** just around the steel gate. This descent, though marred by fallen trees across the trail, should revive and invigorate your spirit for speed!
3.4	0.2	★ Overlook to the left at the burned out campfires.
5.8	2.4	Continue **straight** around the gate.
6.5	0.7	Turn **left** onto **PINE SWAMP RD**.
7.0	0.5	**Cross** a small bridge, then turn **left** onto **LAUREL RUN RD**. Begin the climb back to the top. Like skiing, in order to take a great downhill run, you must first take the slow lift up.
7.1	0.1	Pass **Owl Gap** hunting lodge on the right.
10.9	3.8	You've nearly reached the summit, but first, turn **right** through the gate and up to the **FIRE TOWER**. The view of Happy Valley is outstanding.

11.9	1.0	★ Reach the **FIRE TOWER**. What a view! Go back down to **Laurel Run Rd**.
12.9	1.0	Turn **right** onto **LAUREL RUN RD**. Start the descent to the bottom.
15.4	2.5	Turn **left** onto **BEAR MEADOWS RD**.
15.8	0.4	**BEAR MEADOWS RD** becomes pavement.
16.0	0.2	Arrive at **Tussey Mtn Ski Area**. Maybe the lounge is open for drinks. Check it out!

6. BEAR MEADOWS

Start: *Tussey Mountain Ski Area*	**Total Elevation Gain:** *1390 feet*
Length: *14.2 miles*	**Riding Time:** *1-1½ hours*
Rating: *Moderate to Difficult*	**Calories Burned:** *600-1000*

Pedal through Galbreth Gap to the summit of Thickhead Mountain where a stunning view of Bear Meadows awaits you. This "Registered Natural Landmark" is home to specimens of trees and shrubs not found anywhere else in Pennsylvania. Bear Meadows' 325 acres is described as a "botanist's paradise," with black and red spruce, balsam fir, pitcher plants, sundew, and tree huckleberry growing naturally in the area.

A quick and exhilarating descent brings you to the landmark's entrance and hiking trail, which is a highly recommended diversion. Please be considerate to hikers and the Mid State Trail by walking or riding your bike through the Meadows slowly and cautiously.

The rest of the way down to the ski area zips you along on what is called "The Magic Carpet Ride," a grassy trail winding around to the base of Tussey Mountain.

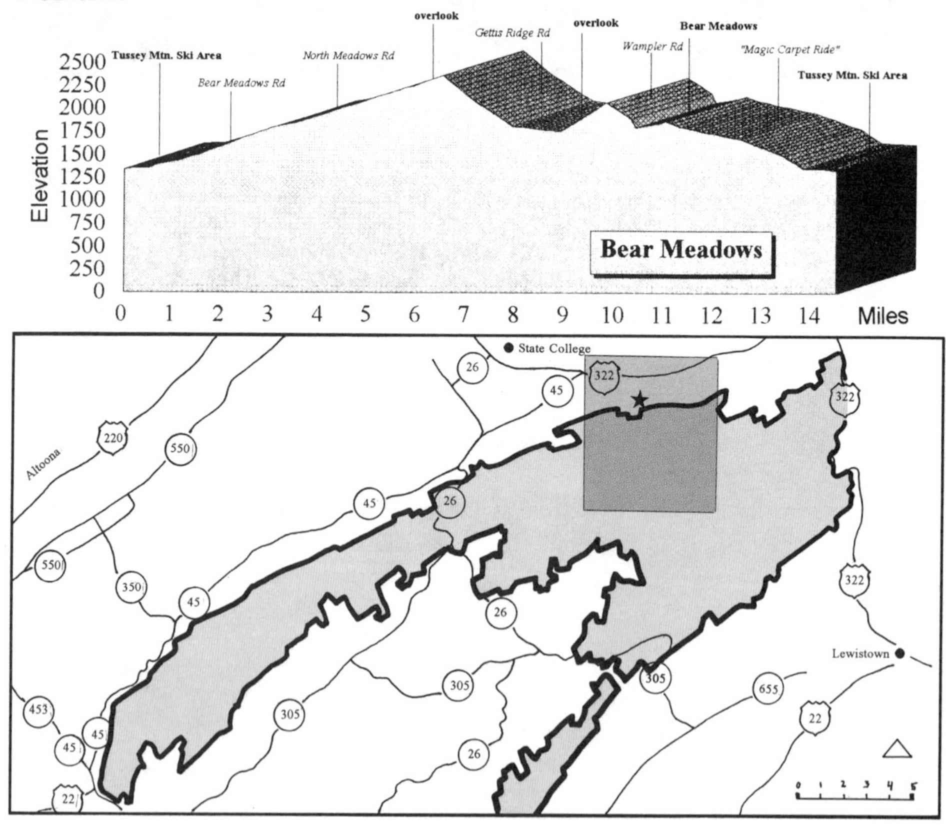

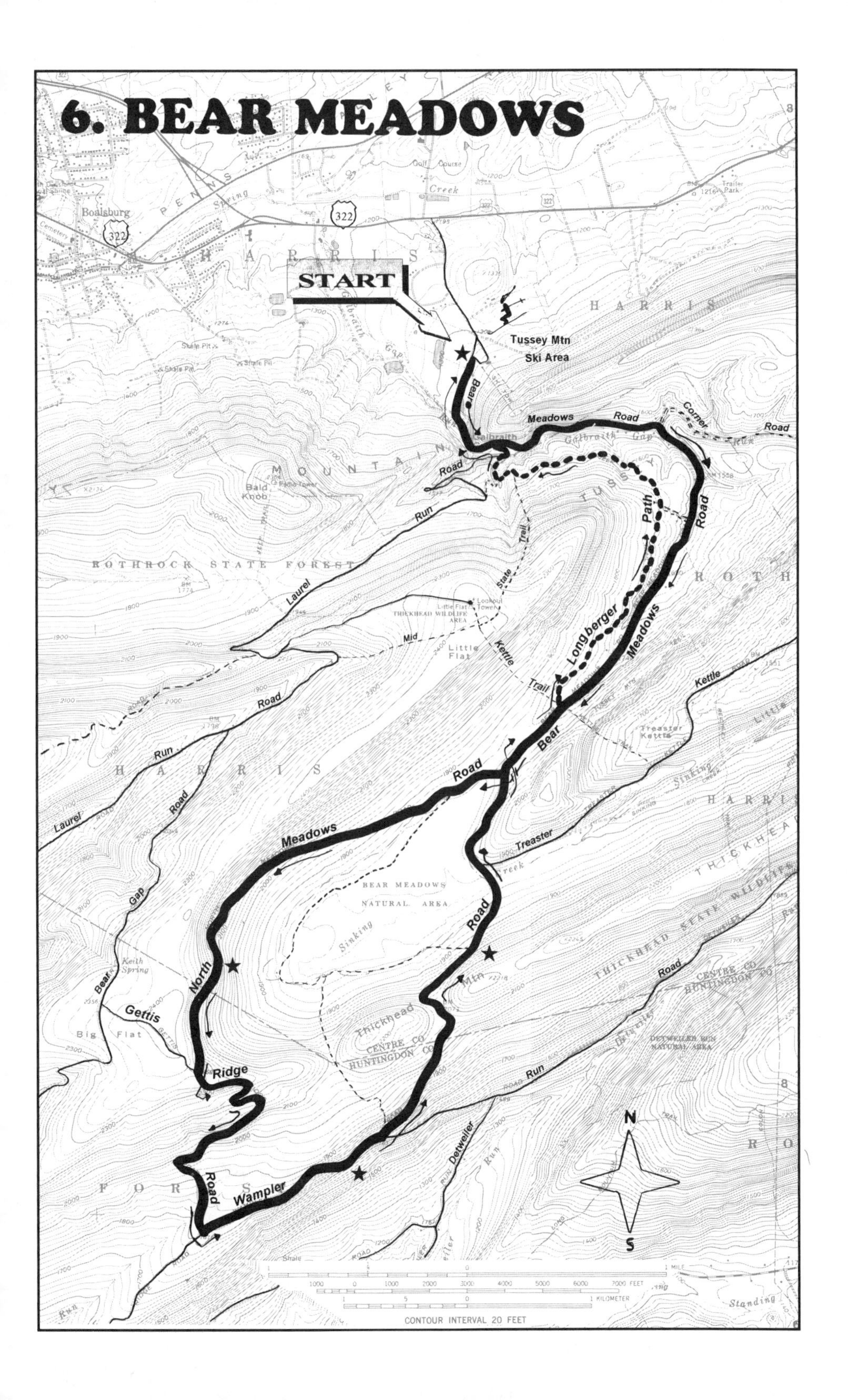

6. BEAR MEADOWS
START
Boalsburg
322
Tussey Mtn
Ski Area
Bear
Meadows
Road
Galbraith
Road
Corner
Road
Path
Longberger
Meadows
Bear
Road
Meadows
North
Ridge
Road
Wampler
Road
Laurel
Run
Mid
State
Trail
Kettle
Trail
Bald Knob
ROTHROCK STATE FOREST
Little Flat
BEAR MEADOWS
NATURAL AREA
Treaster
Kettle
Gap
Gettis
Big Flat
Keith Spring
Thickhead
CENTRE CO
HUNTINGDON CO
Detweiler
Run
N
S
CONTOUR INTERVAL 20 FEET

Bear Meadows

Where To Begin ☞ *Tussey Mtn Ski Area, just off Rte. 322, 6 miles east of State College*

MILES	DISTANCE	DIRECTIONS
0.0	0.0	**START** at the base of **Tussey Mountain**, pedaling your way into the forest along **BEAR MEADOWS RD.**
0.1	0.1	The pavement on **BEAR MEADOWS RD** deteriorates into a pothole-filled dirt/asphalt road.
0.3	0.2	**Cross** the first **one-lane bridge**.
0.5	0.2	**Cross** the second **one-lane bridge**. Begin climbing up Tussey Mountain.
0.7	0.2	Pass **Laurel Run Rd** on the right. Continue up **BEAR MEADOWS RD**.
1.5	0.8	Pass **Corner Rd** on the left.
2.7	1.2	**BEAR MEADOWS RD** changes to gravel.
3.1	0.4	Pass by a "**Notice**" sign and a line of large boulders on the right. **Remember this spot!** This is the entrance to one of the trails you will be taking later in this ride.
3.5	0.4	Turn **right** onto **NORTH MEADOWS RD**. This is where the real climbing begins.
5.3	1.8	★ Scenic vista on the left overlooking **Bear Meadows**.
5.9	0.6	Reach the summit of **Bell Ridge Mtn**. Turn **left** onto **RIDGE RD**.
7.3	1.4	Turn **left** onto **WAMPLER RD**.
8.1	0.8	★ Scenic vista on the right. The view from here is absolutely incredible!

8.3	0.2	Bear **left** at the fork in the road, continuing up **WAMPLER RD**.
9.2	0.9	Reach the summit of **Thickhead Mountain**. Start a fast descent.
9.8	0.6	★ Reach the bottom of the descent, cross a small bridge, and arrive at **Bear Meadows National Natural Landmark**.
10.5	0.5	Stay **left** on **WAMPLER RD**. Pass **Treaster Kettle Rd** at the intersection.
10.7	0.4	Bear **right**, continuing on **BEAR MEADOWS RD**.
11.1	0.4	Turn **left** onto **LONGBERGER PATH** at the **boulders** and "**Notice**" signs. This is a grassy trail wrapping around the northern base of Greenlee Mountain. Bear **right** immediately on this trail. Don't follow **Kettle trail**, which goes straight up the mountain.
12.2	1.1	Pass a hunting lodge on the left.
13.1	0.9	Come to a trail intersection. Following the trail posts, turn **right**, continuing downhill. Turning left will take you straight up to the firetower.
13.3	0.2	Cross the stream at the white cabin.
13.4	0.1	Turn **right** onto **LAUREL RUN RD**.
13.5	0.1	Turn **left** onto **BEAR MEADOWS RD**, going downhill toward **Tussey Mountain Ski Area**.
14.2	0.7	Return to the base of the slopes. Step into the lodge for a few striff drinks and a snack after that ride.

7. GREENWOOD FURNACE

Start: *Greenwood Furnace State Park*
Length: *14.8 miles*
Rating: *Moderate to Difficult*
Total Elevation Gain: *1464 feet*
Riding Time: *1-1½ hours*
Calories Burned: *600-1000*

There are plenty of great things to see as this ride takes you up and around Broad Mountain. Starting in Greenwood Furnace, home of 19th century iron furnaces, you will travel along forest roads to the nearby Alan Seeger Natural Area. This beautiful area was named in honor of a young American poet whose life was lost in World War I.

For those who have never seen virgin hemlock or white pine, the sight is impressive. These tall trees dominate Alan Seeger's landscape in unequaled beauty. Stretch your legs up the mountain climb and you'll be rewarded with a 360° view of the world around you from Greenwood's fire tower. Only an airplane can give a better view. On your way down the other side, keep your eyes peeled for the dense growth of rhododendron along Standing Stone Creek. These bloom in July and make the trip well worth the effort.

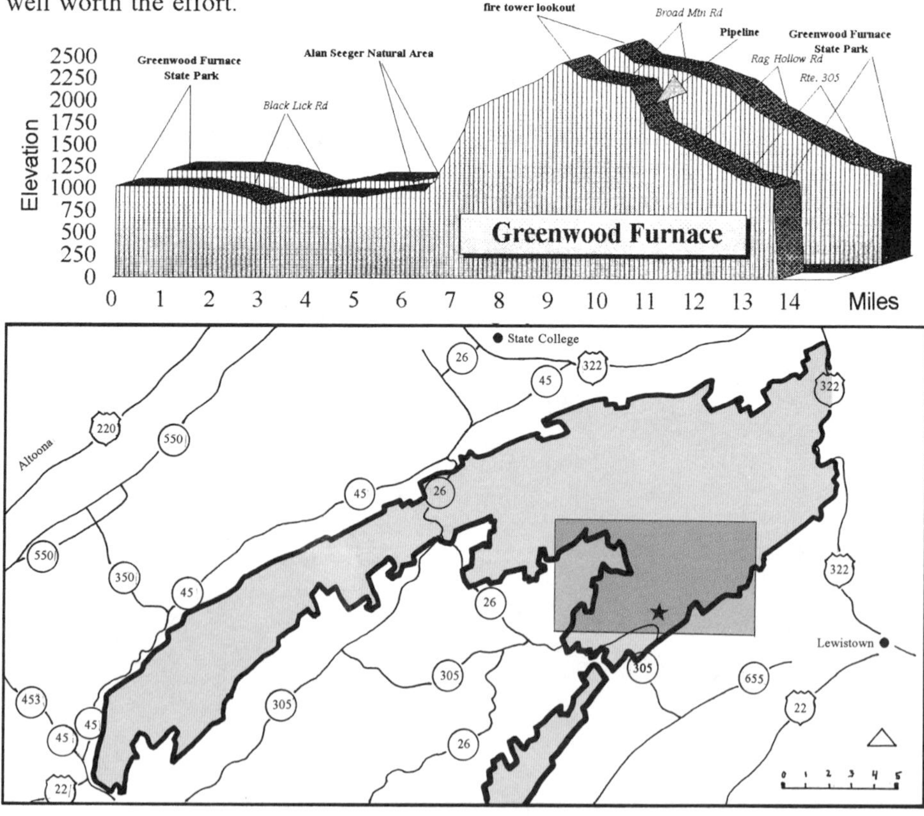

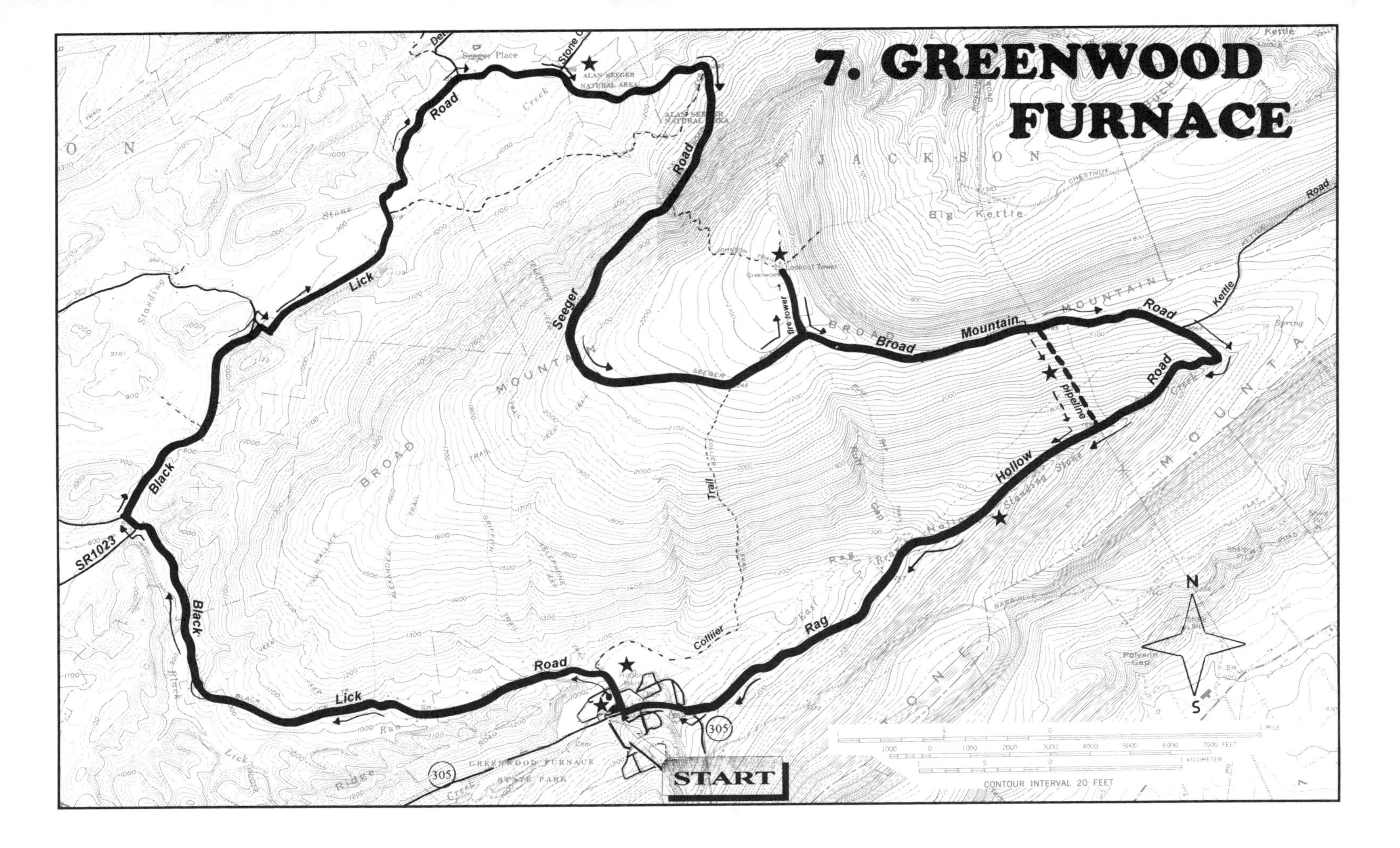

7. GREENWOOD FURNACE
START
Seeger Road
Lick Road
Black Lick Road
Broad Mountain Road
Kettle Road
Hollow Road
Rag Hollow Road
Seeger Place
Stone Creek
ALAN SEEGER NATURAL AREA
fire tower
pipeline
Collier Trail
SR1023
305
Big Kettle
J A C K S O N
B R O A D
M O U N T A I N
Standing Stone
GREENWOOD FURNACE STATE PARK
Polyann Gap
N
S
CONTOUR INTERVAL 20 FEET
1 MILE
1 KILOMETER

Greenwood Furnace

Where To Begin ☞ *Greenwood Furnace State Park. just off Rte. 305, 10 minutes west of Belleville, 40 minutes southeast of State College*

MILES	DISTANCE	DIRECTIONS
0.0	0.0	**START** at **Greenwood Furnace State Park**. Turn **left** from the information center parking lot onto **BLACK LICK RD**. Follow the signs toward **Alan Seeger Natural Area**.
0.1	0.1	★ Pass the historic **Greenwood Works furnace** on the right. The Furnace was in operation from 1834 to 1904.
0.2	0.1	Bear **left** at the fork, continuing on **BLACK LICK RD**. **Collier Trail** is on the right.
1.4	1.2	Pass the **Great Oaks** camp on the left.
3.0	1.6	Turn **right** at the stop sign onto paved road.
3.1	0.1	Turn **right** off of the pavement following signs to **Alan Seeger Natural Area**.
4.1	1.0	Bear **right.**
4.2	0.1	Bear **left**.
5.1	0.9	**Cross** a **one-lane bridge.**
5.3	0.2	**BLACK LICK RD** turns to pavement once again. Re-enter **Rothrock State Forest** under a canopy of tall white pines.
5.9	0.6	Bear **right** toward **Alan Seeger Natural Area**.
6.4	0.5	Cross the small bridge and enter **Alan Seeger Natural Area**. Turn **right**, heading for **SEEGER RD** and **Greenwood Furnace** signs. Start climbing this long, steep climb.

8.8	2.4	Reach the summit. Turn **left** and climb up to the **fire tower.**
9.15	0.35	★ Reach the fire tower. Climb to the top and get a 360° view of Rothrock State Forest. You can clearly see the fire towers from other mountains in the area poking into the sky.
9.5	0.35	Return to the mountain road. Turn **left** on what is now **BROAD MOUNTAIN RD**. Begin the descent down the other side of the mountain.
10.6	1.1	Cross the **pipe line**.
		★ For those of you bold enough to go for it, turn **right** and take the awesome descent down the **pipeline**, 0.4 miles long. It takes you down to **RAG HOLLOW RD** where you must turn **right** toward **Greenwood Furnace**.
11.6	1.0	Hairpin turn. **BROAD MOUNTAIN RD** turns into **RAG HOLLOW RD**.
12.2	0.6	Cross the **pipe line** at the bottom end. Go for it next time!
14.5	2.3	Reach the bottom of this descent. Turn **right** at the stop sign, heading back to **Greenwood Furnace State Park**.
14.8	0.3	Turn **right** off of the road and you're back at the information center. Ask the information center how much food you will need to consume after that ride.

8. COLYER LAKE

Start: *Colyer Lake*	**Total Elevation Gain:** *1450 feet*
Length: *14.3 miles*	**Riding Time:** *1-1½ hours*
Rating: *Moderate to Difficult*	**Calories Burned:** *800-1500*

This is a great ride to do while on a day trip to Colyer Lake. With all of the relaxing that's so common at Colyer Lake, you might feel the need for speed and a bit of activity. Get started by pedaling through Boal Gap and up Sand Mountain to check out the wildlife and the beauty from above the lake. The uphill singletrack will challenge you, and the zip back down the other side will exhilarate you. Have fun cycling from Colyer Lake!

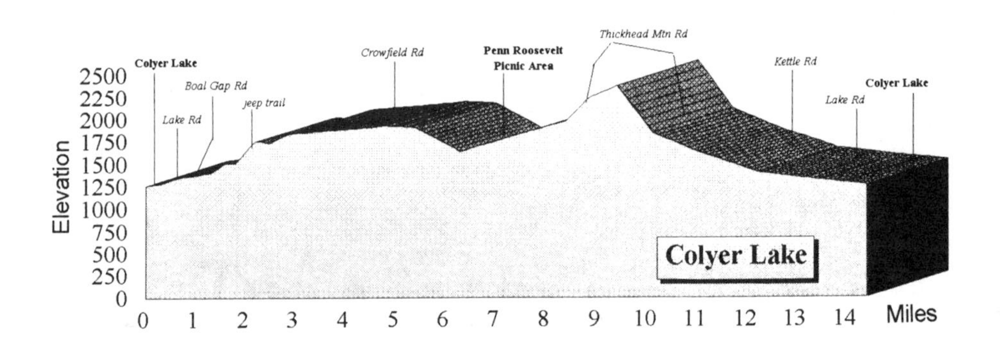

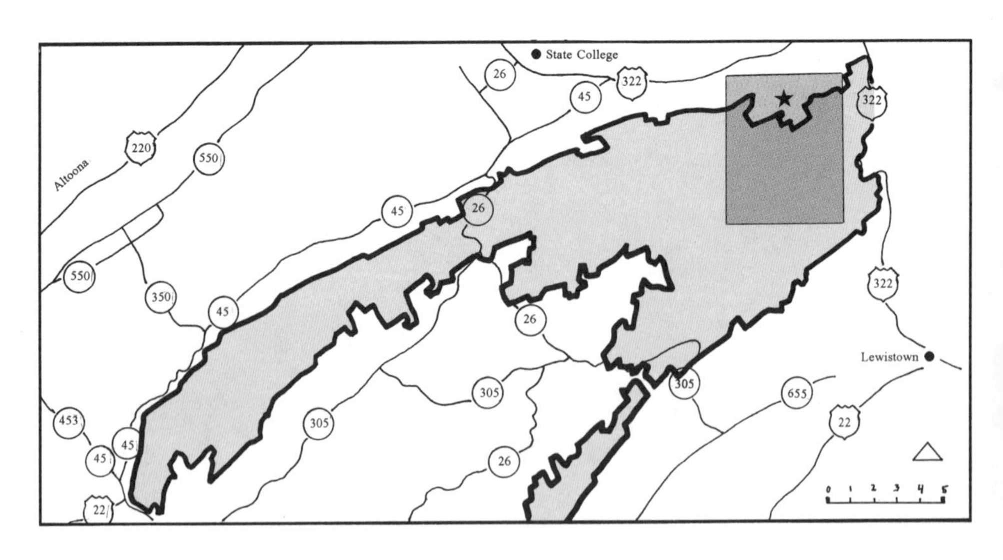

8. COLYER LAKE

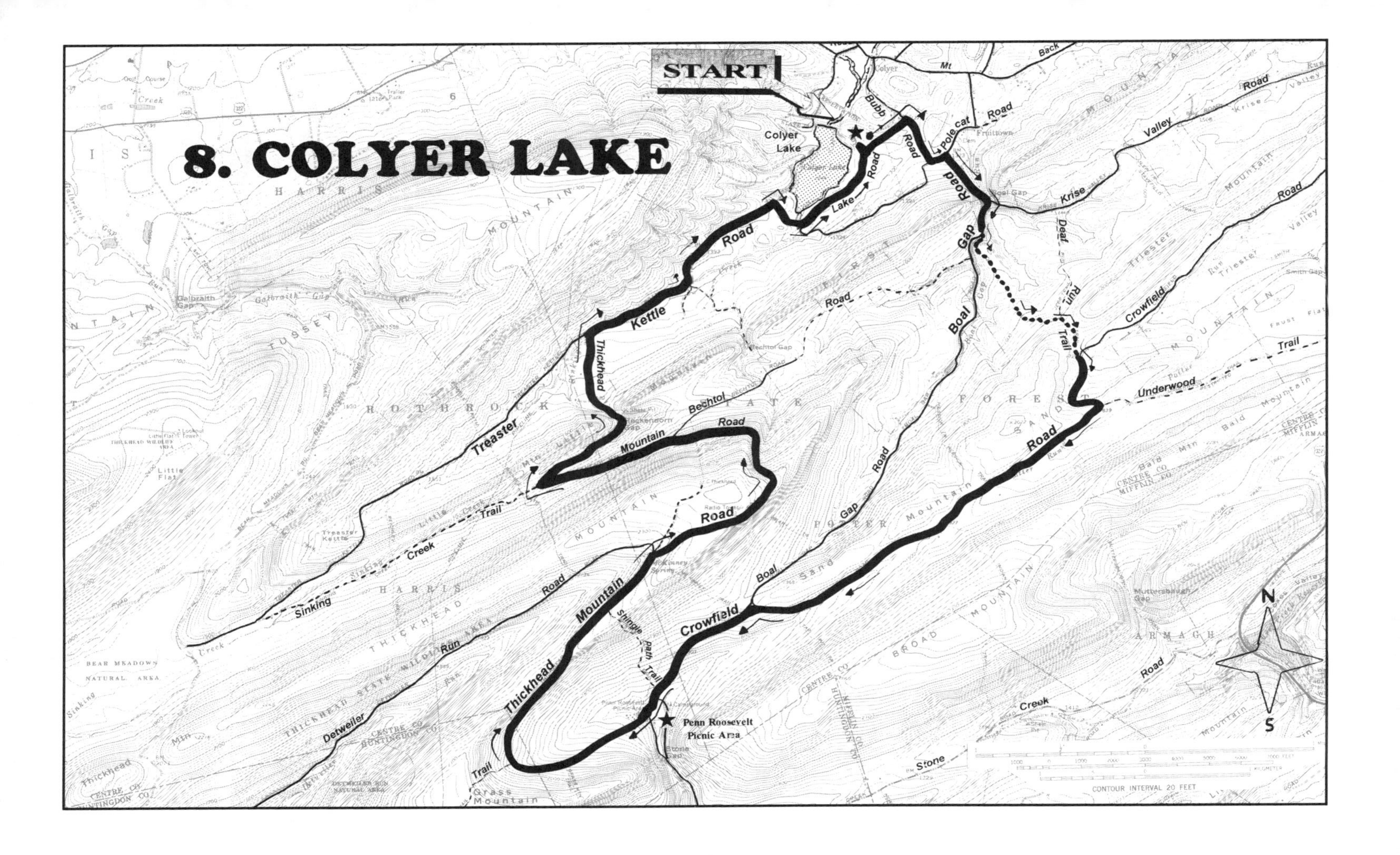

Colyer Lake

Where To Begin ☞ *Colyer Lake, south of Rte. 322, 9 miles east of State College*

MILES	DISTANCE	DIRECTIONS
0.0	0.0	**START** from the east side of **Colyer Lake** at the small parking lot just off of **Lake Rd**. Turn **left** from the parking lot, heading east on **LAKE RD**.
0.3	0.3	Turn **right** onto **BUBB RD**.
0.6	0.3	Turn **left** onto **POLECAT RD**.
0.7	0.1	Turn **right** onto **BOAL GAP RD**, heading toward the mountain through Boal Gap.
0.9	0.2	**BOAL GAP RD** turns to gravel.
1.1	0.2	Pass **Krise Valley Rd** on the left. Continue on **BOAL GAP RD**.
1.3	0.2	Following the overhead telephone lines, turn **left** off **BOAL GAP RD** into the woods. Cross the stream here.
		!! There is a steep hill just across the stream. Follow the trail up this hill.
1.75	0.45	Come to a cleared area. Cross this area toward the shale and gravel covered road.
1.8	0.05	Immediately crossing this area, turn **right** off of this shale-gravel road onto a grassy **JEEP TRAIL**. **Keep your eyes open for this!!** Follow the trail marked with **blue double (=) lines.**
1.85	0.05	At the little intersection in this trail bear **right**, continuing up the **JEEP TRAIL** with the double-blue-line trail markers. This trail starts going straight up.
2.1	0.25	Bear **right** at this intersection, continuing up. **Deaf Run Jeep Trail** is to the left.

2.2	0.1	Reach the summit of this trail.
2.5	0.3	The trail turns into a gravel road. Continue **straight**, then bear **right** onto **CROWFIELD RD**.
2.9	0.4	Reach the high point (1927 ft) of this seemingly endless climb. Stay **right**, continuing on **CROWFIELD RD**.
5.4	2.5	Come to the intersection with **Boal Gap Rd**. Bear **left**, continuing on **CROWFIELD RD**.
6.3	0.9	Bottom of descent.
		★ **Penn Roosevelt Picnic Area and lake**. Stop for a rest.
		Take the first **right** off of **Crowfield Rd**, heading up **THICKHEAD MOUNTAIN RD**. This is a rocky jeep trail that starts just across from the Penn Roosevelt stone furnace.
6.5	0.2	Go around the steel gate. Continue the climb upward.
8.3	1.8	Pass **Shinglepath Trail** on the right.
8.8	0.5	Come to a 3-way intersection. Bear **right**, continuing on **THICKHEAD MOUNTAIN RD**.
9.9	1.1	Go around the boulders that block the road. House on the right.
10.0	0.1	Pass **Bechtol Rd** on the right.
10.8	0.8	Go through the switchback, heading toward **Heckendorn Gap**.
12.1	1.3	Turn **right** onto **TREASTER KETTLE RD**.
12.8	0.7	Turn **left** at ╣, continuing on **TREASTER KETTLE RD**. There is a house on the right at this intersection.
13.6	0.8	Bear **right** following the main road.

13.8	0.2	Turn **left** onto **LAKE RD**.
14.3	0.5	Arrive at the parking lot and your car. Time to pull up a lawn chair and watch the boaters zip around the lake.

Bald Eagle State Forest

Over one-third of Bald Eagle's nearly 200,000 acres is a watershed, emptying its many streams into the Susquehanna River. Its boundaries stretch through Centre, Mifflin, Snyder, Union, Clinton, and Lycoming Counties, lying in Pennsylvania's beautiful region of rolling ridges and valleys. The proper use, management, and care of this delicate land is essential.

This state forest was named for the great Indian chief Bald Eagle, and is bordered in the northernmost section by the vast west branch of the Susquehanna River. Forty-seven miles of some of the finest trout fishing streams in the nation feed into this great river. Trout fishermen from around the country travel to these streams to angle for a record catch, including former president Jimmy Carter. Twenty-seven vistas look out over Bald Eagle State Forest, offering spectacular views of the deep valleys below where countless game animals of all major species coexist.

Bald Eagle is host to four state parks: Reeds Gap State Park; Poe Valley State Park (legend has it that this region is named for an early pioneer thought to be Edgar Allen Poe's cousin); Snyder-Middleswarth State Park, home of the largest original-growth big timber in Pennsylvania; and R.B. Winter State Park, with swimming and fishing at Halfway Lake.

There are a number of natural areas in Bald Eagle worth noting as well: Joyce Kilmer Natural Area boasts 77 acres of virgin white pine and hemlock; Hook Natural Area has over 5,000 acres of preserved watershed; Tall Timbers Natural Area near Snyder-Middleswarth State Park; Rosencrans Bog, a high-mountain bog with cranberry, mountain holly, and blueberry; and White Mountain Wild Area along Penns Creek, its slopes formed by weather resistant sandstone bleached white by the sun.

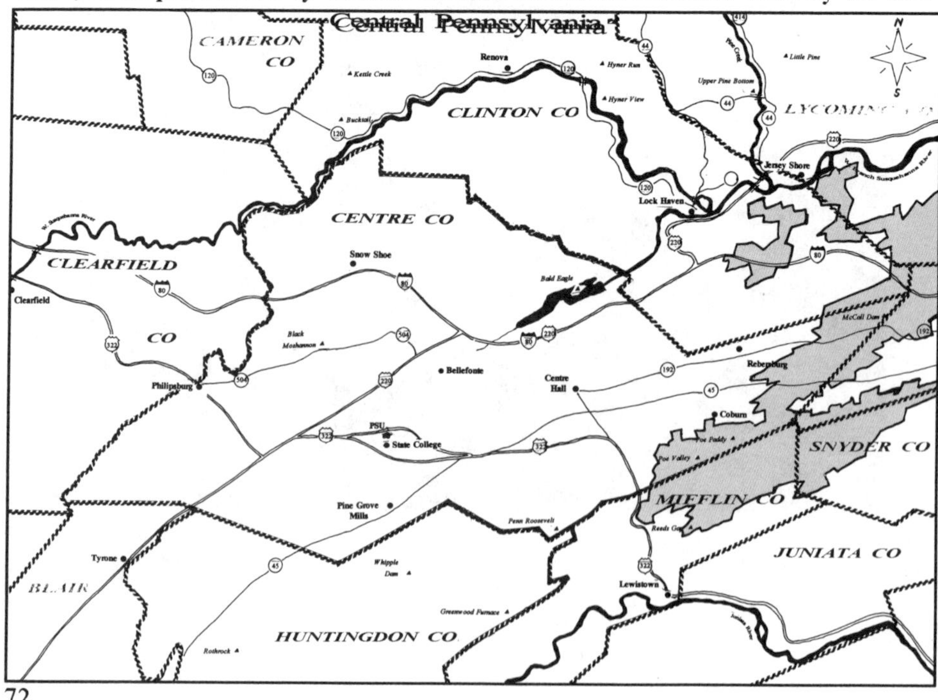

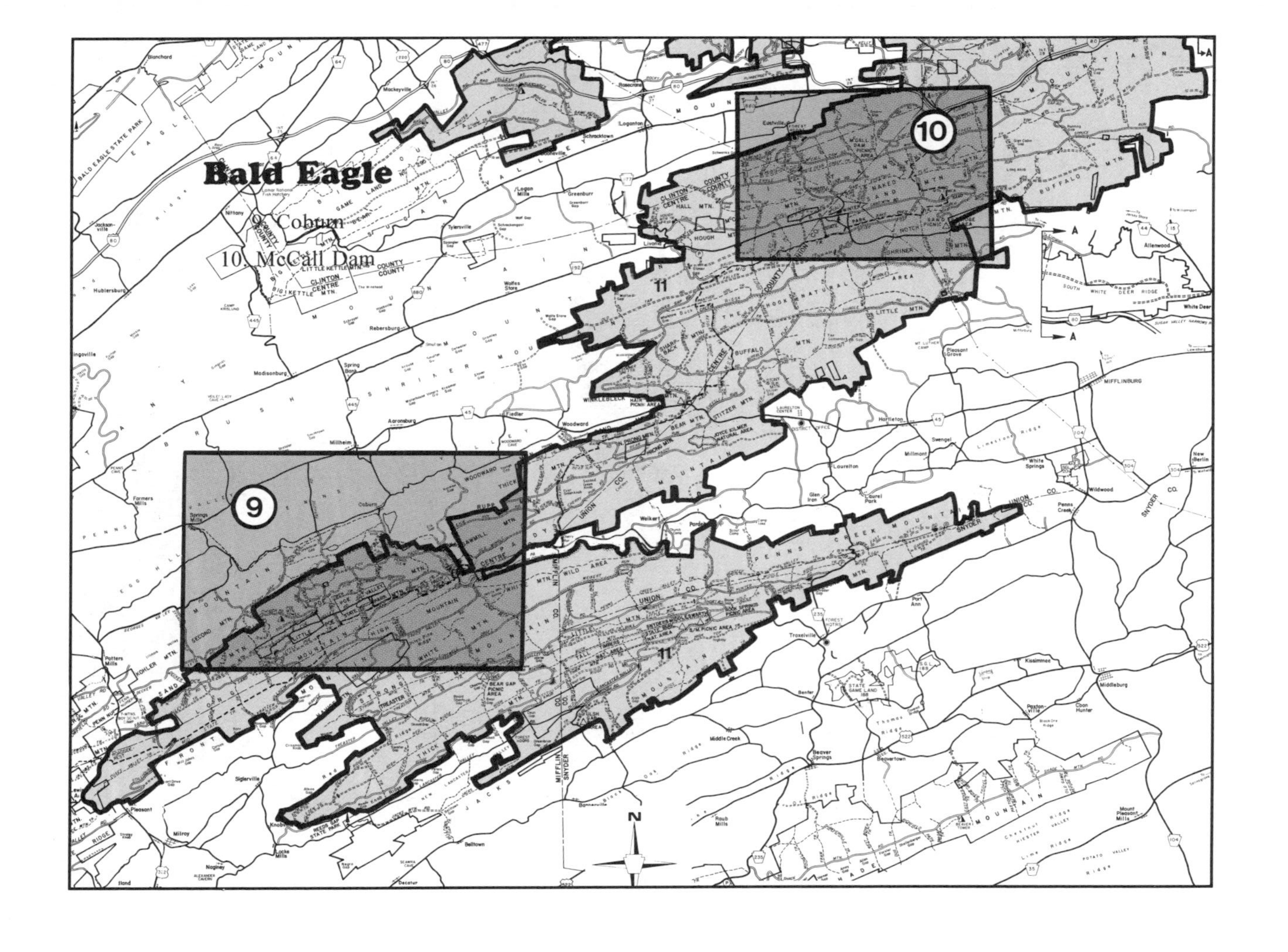

Bald Eagle
Coburn
10. McCall Dam
10
9
11
11
N
A
A
Blanchard
Mackeyville
Loganton
Nittany
Tylersville
Greenburr
Logan Mills
Hublersburg
Jacksonville
Rebersburg
Madisonburg
Spring Bank
Aaronsburg
Millheim
Woodward
Fiedler
Wolfes Store
Farmers Mills
Springs Mills
Potters Mills
Siglerville
Milroy
Belltown
Decatur
Knob
Locke Mills
Reeds Gap State Park
Laurelton
Weikert
Glen Iron
Laurel Park
Millmont
Swengel
Hartleton
Mifflinburg
White Springs
Wildwood
New Berlin
Penns Creek
Troxelville
Port Ann
Kissimmee
Middleburg
Beaver Springs
Beavertown
Middle Creek
Raub Mills
Bannerville
Mount Pleasant Mills
Allenwood
White Deer
Pleasant Grove
Troxelville
Benfer
Peyton-ville
Coon Hunter
BALD EAGLE STATE PARK
SOUTH WHITE DEER RIDGE
WINKLEBLECK
BUFFALO MTN.
SHRINER
LITTLE MTN.
PENNS CREEK MOUNTAIN
JOYCE KILMER NATURAL AREA
BEAR GAP PICNIC AREA
TREASTER
CLINTON COUNTY
CENTRE COUNTY
UNION CO.
SNYDER CO.
MIFFLIN CO.

9. COBURN

Start: *Coburn Schoolhouse*	**Total Elevation Gain:** *984 feet*
Length: *16.3 miles*	**Riding Time:** *1-1½ hours*
Rating: *Moderate*	**Calories Burned:** *800-1200*

This ride is inspired by one of Central Pennsylvania's greatest bike racing events, *The Coburn Mountain Bike Race*. Twice a year hundreds of mountain bike enthusiasts come to test their strength and will against Bald Eagle's rugged terrain. They climb the mountains, cross the streams, race down kamikaze singletrack, through tunnels, over narrow train trestles, and they all love every minute of it. Or so they say a few days later. Many of the roads and trails on this ride are part of the *Coburn* bike race course. Of course, don't feel that you have to race it. This ride is so beautiful, it would be a shame to miss anything at all.

Once you've climbed to the top of Little Poe Mountain, the rest of the ride is all downhill. Enjoy the scenery, the roads along the water, and the unique adventure of riding through abandoned Railroad tunnels and over Penns Creek on wooden trestles. There's much more to this ride than a great race.

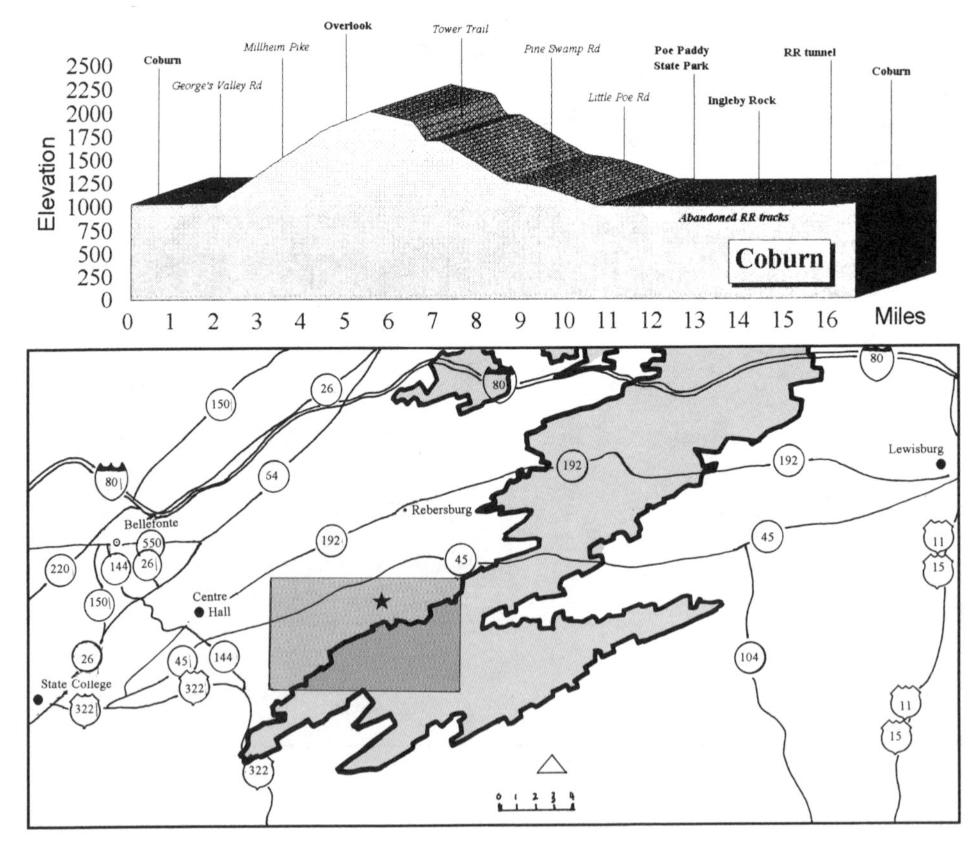

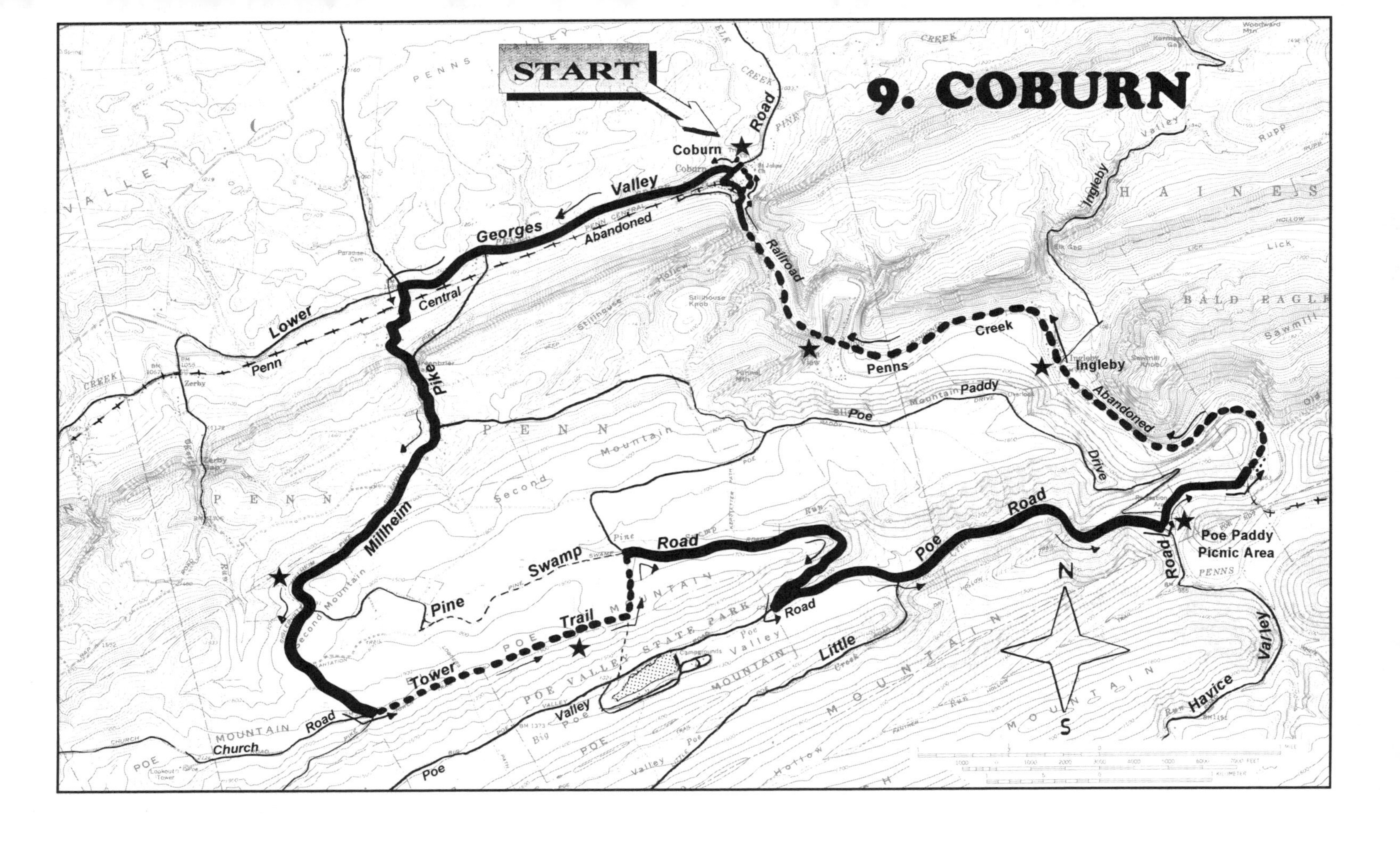
9. COBURN
START
Coburn
Road
Georges
Valley
Abandoned
Railroad
Central
Lower
Penn
Pike
Millheim
Penns
Creek
Ingleby
Abandoned
Mountain
Paddy
Poe
Drive
Poe
Road
Poe Paddy
Picnic Area
Road
Pine
Swamp
Road
Road
Tower
Trail
Pine
Little
Havice
Valley
Road
Church
N
S

Coburn

Where To Begin ☞ *Town of Coburn, south of Rte. 45, 18 miles east of State College, just below Millheim*

MILES	DISTANCE	DIRECTIONS
0.0	0.0	**START** at the **Penn Township School** parking lot. Turn **left** onto **GEORGES VALLEY RD (Main St)**.
0.1	0.1	Bear **right** at the bridge, continuing on **GEORGES VALLEY RD**.
2.0	1.9	Turn **left** onto **MILLHEIM PIKE**, crossing the bridge over Penns Creek.
4.2	2.2	★ Scenic vista on the right.
4.4	0.2	Pass **Pine Swamp Rd** on the left.
5.2	0.8	Reach the summit of this climb. Turn **left** off the road through a gate onto **TOWER TRAIL**. This is a rocky singletrack mountain trail. The descent is very fast, bumpy, and technical.
6.2	1.0	Start descending. Hold onto your lunch on this one!
6.5	0.3	Reach the bottom of the descent and turn **left** on the **JEEP TRAIL** toward **Pine Swamp Rd**.
6.8	0.3	Turn **right** onto **PINE SWAMP RD**. Ready for another descent?
8.5	1.7	At the bottom of this descent turn hard **left** onto **BIG POE VALLEY RD**.
		★ Poe Valley State Park is about one mile to the right.
9.2	0.7	Cross over Little Poe Creek. Stay **left** on **LITTLE POE RD**. This is a lovely ride alone the creek.
10.8	1.6	Turn **left** at the large brown "Park" sign into **Poe Paddy State Park** camping area.

		★ Poe Paddy State Park.
10.85	0.05	Cross over a little wooden bridge. At the sign pointing toward Coburn on **Poe Paddy Drive**, turn **RIGHT** instead, heading toward Penns Creek.
11.4	0.55	Come to a little intersection at road's end. Turn **left** toward the three-house town on **RAMSEY LN**. Penns Creek on the right.
12.1	0.7	**Ramsey Rd** comes to an end at the gate. Go around this gate and follow the **ABANDONED RAILROAD BED** along Penns Creek back home to Coburn.
12.4	0.3	Cross the railroad trestle over Penns Creek.
13.6	1.2	Enter the small town of Ingleby.
		★ Be sure to notice **Ingleby Rock** hanging from a tripod in the village "square." This rock is claimed to have mythical Indian powers.
15.0	1.4	Cross the railroad trestle over Penns Creek.
15.1	0.1	★ Go into the tunnel which takes you through Tunnel Mtn. It's going to be dark, so be on guard for other cyclists or hikers.
16.0	0.9	Enter in the outskirts of the town of Coburn. Turn **right** where the road ends toward Penns Creek.
16.1	0.1	You can either turn **right** crossing through the creek, coming out into the park behind the school **or** continue straight along the road and enter Coburn from the front. The latter choice will keep you dry.
16.3	0.2	Whichever route you took, dry or wet, you should be back in this picturesque little town of Coburn.

10. McCALL DAM

Start: *R.B. Winter State Park*	**Total Elevation Gain:** *1670 feet*
Length: *14.4 miles*	**Riding Time:** *1-1½ hours*
Rating: *Moderate to Difficult*	**Calories Burned:** *600-1000*

This ride begins at Halfway Lake in R.B. Winter State Park, named for the District Forester who spent most of his life living and working in this region. Climbing out of the narrows between Mifflinburg and Centre Hall, you'll make your way over McCall Mountain into White Deer Creek valley where the McCall Dam Picnic Area is situated. This little spot between two mountains is a place like no other, where one can go for peace of mind, do some fishing, and just leave all the bad stuff behind. The next climb takes you over Nittany Mountain into the small Amish town of Eastville where you may find Amish and locals mixing cultures at Sugar Valley Church.

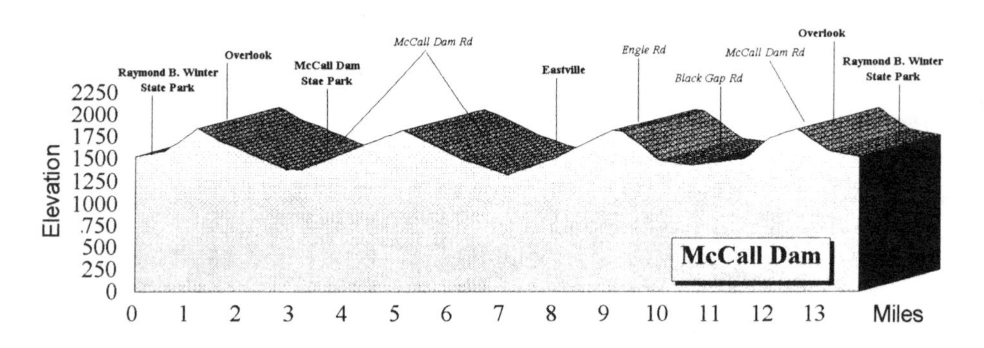

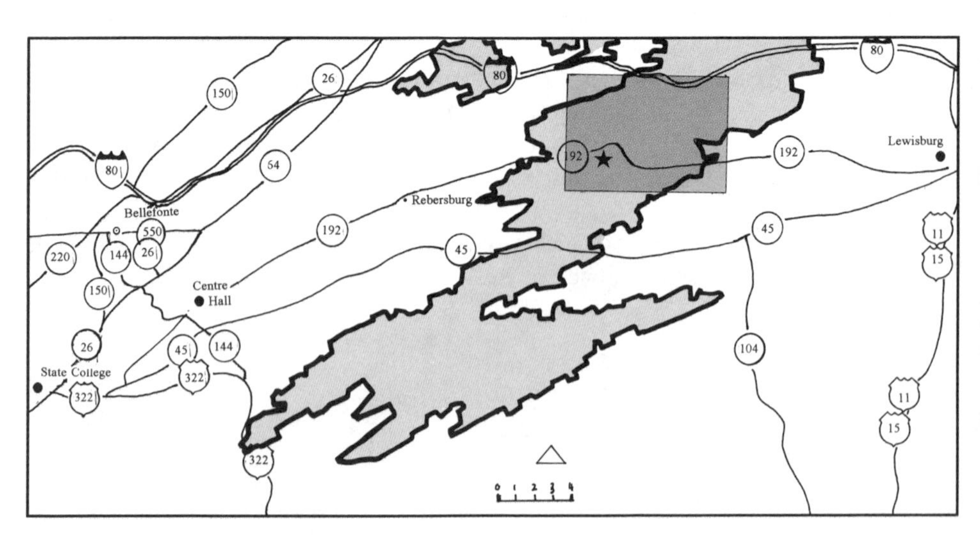

10. McCALL DAM

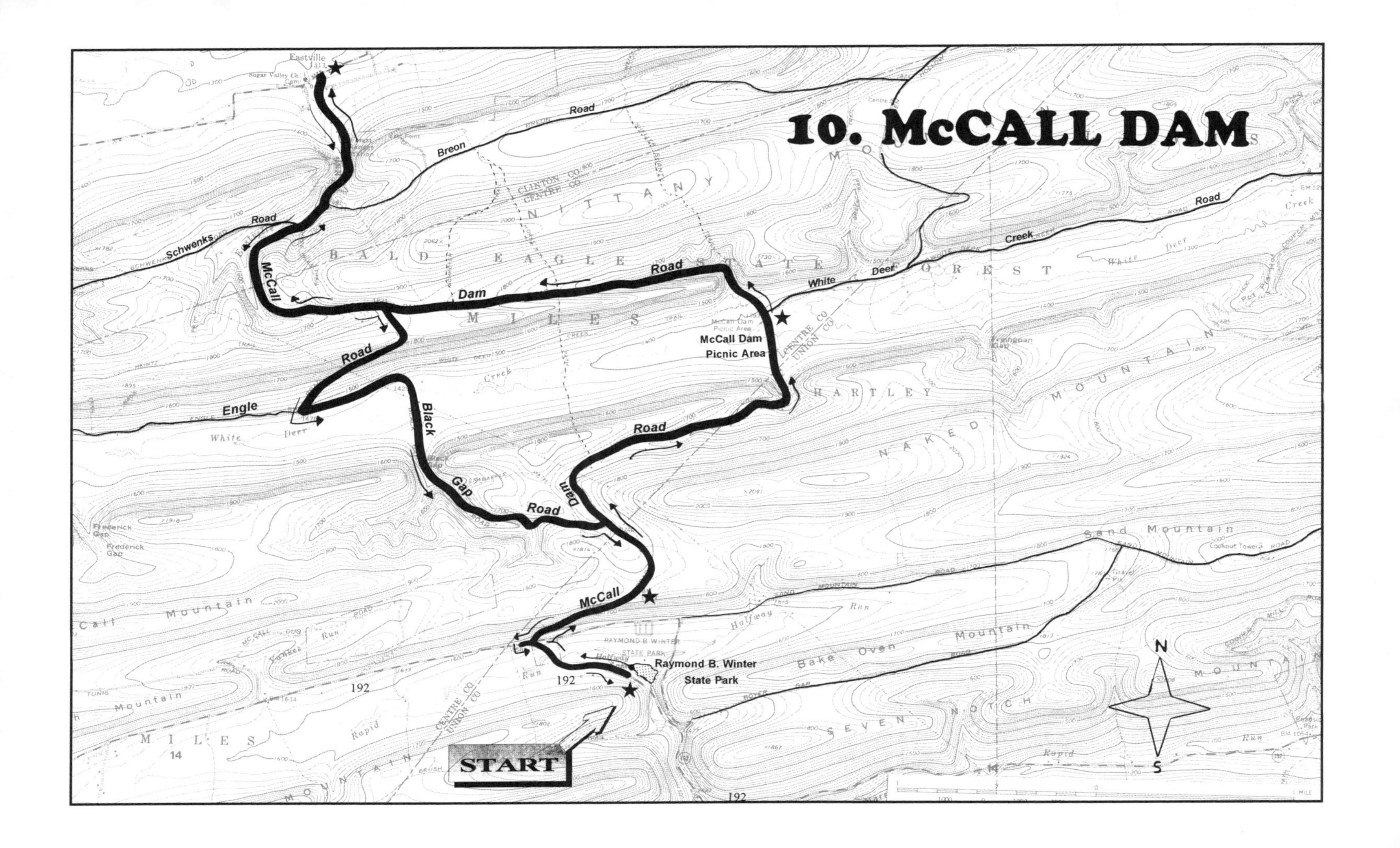

McCall Dam

Where To Begin ☞ *R.B. Winter State Park on the west side of Halfway Lake, 16 miles west of Lewisburg, 20 miles southwest of Lock Haven*

MILES	DISTANCE	DIRECTIONS
0.0	0.0	**START** at **Raymond B. Winter State Park** at the small parking area alongside **Halfway Lake** on **RTE 192**. Head northwest on **RTE 192**.
0.6	0.6	Turn hard **right** toward **McCALL DAM RD**.
0.7	0.1	Bear **right** onto **McCALL DAM RD**.
1.3	0.6	★ Scenic vista on the right overlooking **Halfway Lake**.
1.8	0.5	Stay **right** on **McCALL DAM RD**. **Black Gap Rd** to the left.
2.1	0.3	Cross the **power lines**. Good riding!
2.2	0.1	Pass **Horse Path Trail** on the left. Start descending.
3.6	1.4	Reach the bottom of the descent, cross White Deer Creek and arrive at **McCall Dam Picnic Area.** Continue on **McCALL DAM RD** climbing up Nittany Mountain.
5.6	2.0	Stay **right** on **McCALL DAM RD** descending into Eastville. **Engle Rd** is on the left.
6.7	1.1	**Schwenks Rd** on the left. Continue on **McCALL DAM RD**.
6.9	0.2	**Breon Rd** on the right. Continue on **McCALL DAM RD**.
7.2	0.3	**McCALL DAM RD** turns to pavement.
7.6	0.4	Arrive in the quaint little Amish town of **Eastville**. Do a little shopping before heading back into the hills. Shopping done, head back on **McCALL DAM RD** south toward **Raymond B. Winter State Park**.

8.0	0.4	Pavement ends.
8.3	0.3	**Breon Rd** on the left. Continue on **McCALL DAM RD**.
8.5	0.2	**Schwenks Rd** on the right. Continue on **McCALL DAM RD**.
9.6	1.1	Turn **right** onto **ENGLE RD**. Go around gate if gate is closed. Begin fast descent.
10.5	0.9	Turn **left** onto **BLACK GAP RD** at the bottom of descent.
11.1	0.6	Cross over White Deer Creek.
11.4	0.3	Enter **Black Gap.**
12.1	0.7	Begin steep climb.
12.6	0.5	Top of the climb. Turn **right** onto **McCALL DAM RD**.
13.2	0.6	★ Scenic vista on the left overlooking **Halfway Lake**.
13.8	0.6	Turn hard **left** onto **RTE 192** toward **Raymond B. Winter State Park**.
14.4	0.6	Arrive at **Halfway Lake**. Eat some food, then do some trout fishing while you're here.

The Black Forest

This region in the northeastern section of Central Pennsylvania gets its name from a time when forests here were so dense with hemlock and pine it was tough for even sunlight to shine through. The area was compared to the Black Forest of Germany. Most of that old growth has since disappeared to logging, but virgin pine and hemlock can still be found.

Split along Route 44, Sproul State Forest stretches west as Tiadaghton State Forest runs east. The acquisition of land in Sproul State Forest marks the beginning of the entire state forest system in Pennsylvania, now totalling over 2,000,000 acres. Some of Pennsylvania's most remote and rugged countryside is located in Sproul. Tiadaghton is the name Iroquois Indians gave to Pine Creek, Susquehanna's largest tributary. Pine Creek runs along Pine Creek Gorge through what is known up north in Tioga State Forest as Pennsylvania's "Grand Canyon."

American history was also made in this wilderness region, as a group of people called the Fair Play Settlers set up their own system of government long before Pennsylvania was a part of Union. On July 4th, 1776, the Treaty Elm was signed declaring independence from Great Britain. This was done without the knowledge that the Declaration of Independence was being signed in Philadelphia that same day!

Wildlife of all kinds are abundant in the area, including an occasional rattlesnake. The fantastic Little Pine State Park and the breathtaking Hyner View State Park are keystones of the area, offering outdoors people plenty to do and lots to see in this beautiful and rugged corner of the State called the Black Forest.

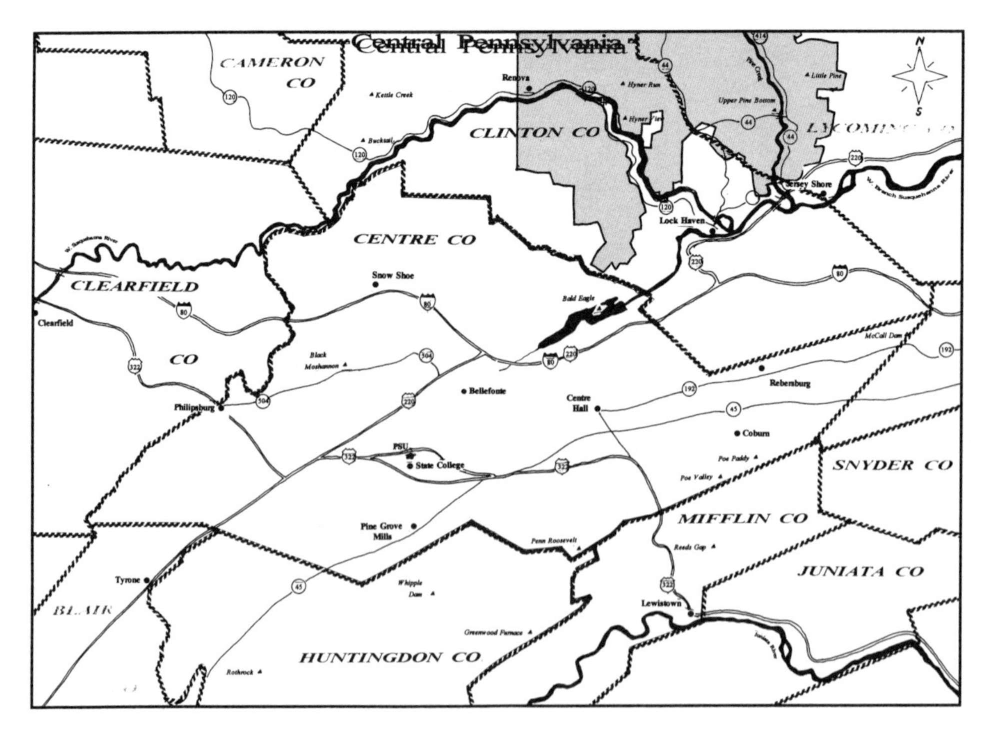

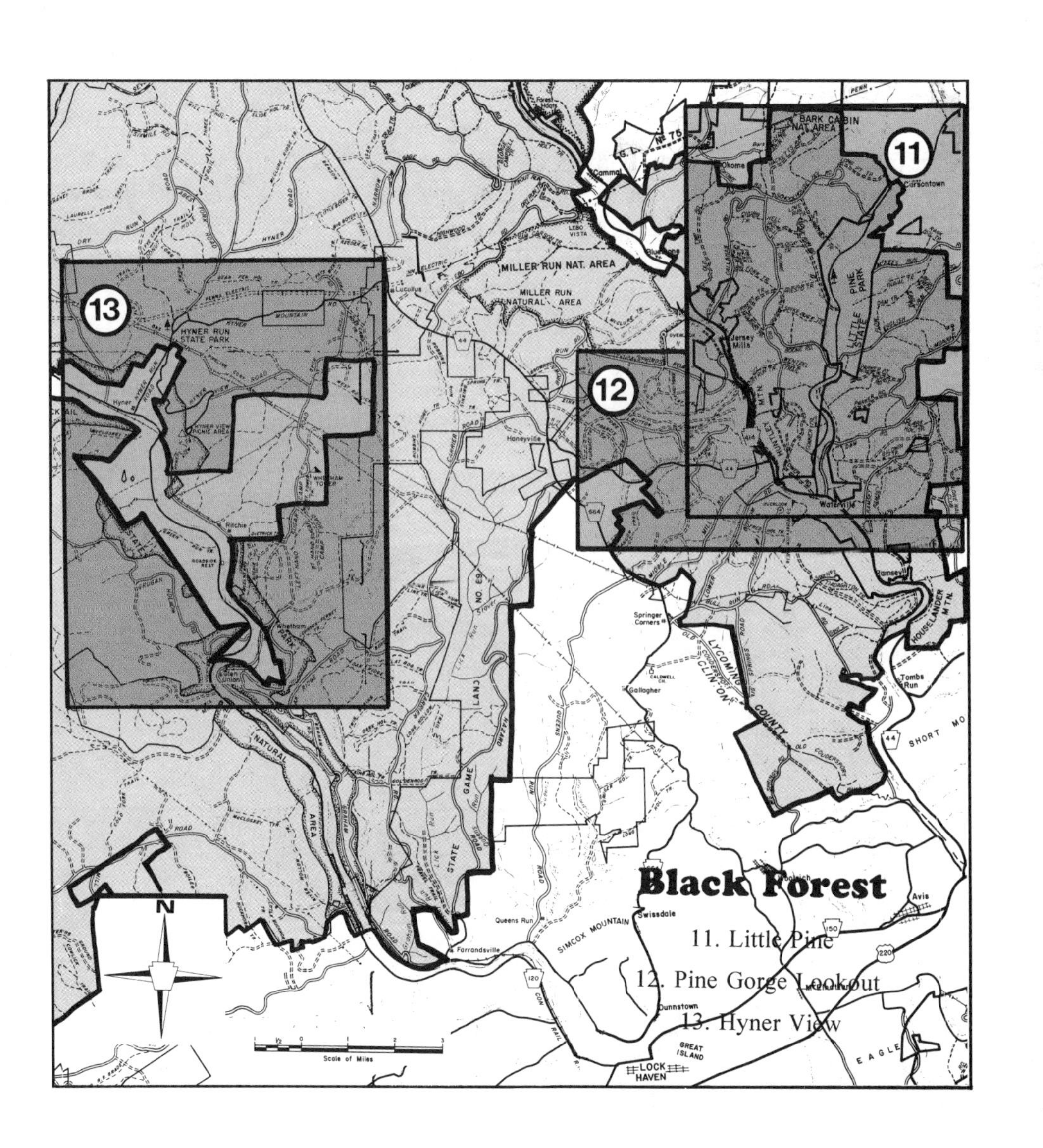

Black Forest
11. Little Pine
12. Pine Gorge Lookout
13. Hyner View
MILLER RUN NAT. AREA
MILLER RUN NATURAL AREA
HYNER RUN STATE PARK
BARK CABIN NAT AREA
LITTLE PINE STATE PARK
Jersey Mills
Waterville
Honeyville
Hyner
Ritchie
Whetham
Springer Corners
Gallagher
Queens Run
Farrandsville
Swissdale
SIMCOX MOUNTAIN
Dunnstown
GREAT ISLAND
LOCK HAVEN
Avis
Tombs Run
HOUSELANDER MTN.
LYCOMING
CLINTON
COUNTY
STATE GAME LAND NO. 89
NATURAL AREA
N
Scale of Miles

11. LITTLE PINE

Start: Little Pine State Park	**Total Elevation Gain:** 1393 feet
Length: 11.7 miles	**Riding Time:** 1-1½ hours
Rating: Moderate	**Calories Burned:** 600-1000

Little Pine State Park is so much more than just a place to come and ride. Constructed by the Civilian Conservation Corps (CCC), Little Pine State Park has grown from a small picnic area along Little Pine Creek to a 2158-acre state park with a 94-acre lake, beach, boating, fishing, campgrounds, hiking trails, and even ice skating. Considered to be in one of the most beautiful mountain sections in the Appalachian region, this is a fantastic place to spend a weekend.

This ride begins at the dam and takes you up Huntley Mountain high above Little Pine. The wilderness of Tiadaghton State Forest gives you an eyeful of some of nature's finest handiwork. After your ride, stop at Happy Acres Clown Lounge for delicious "steak for two" and buy some gifts from the gift shop.

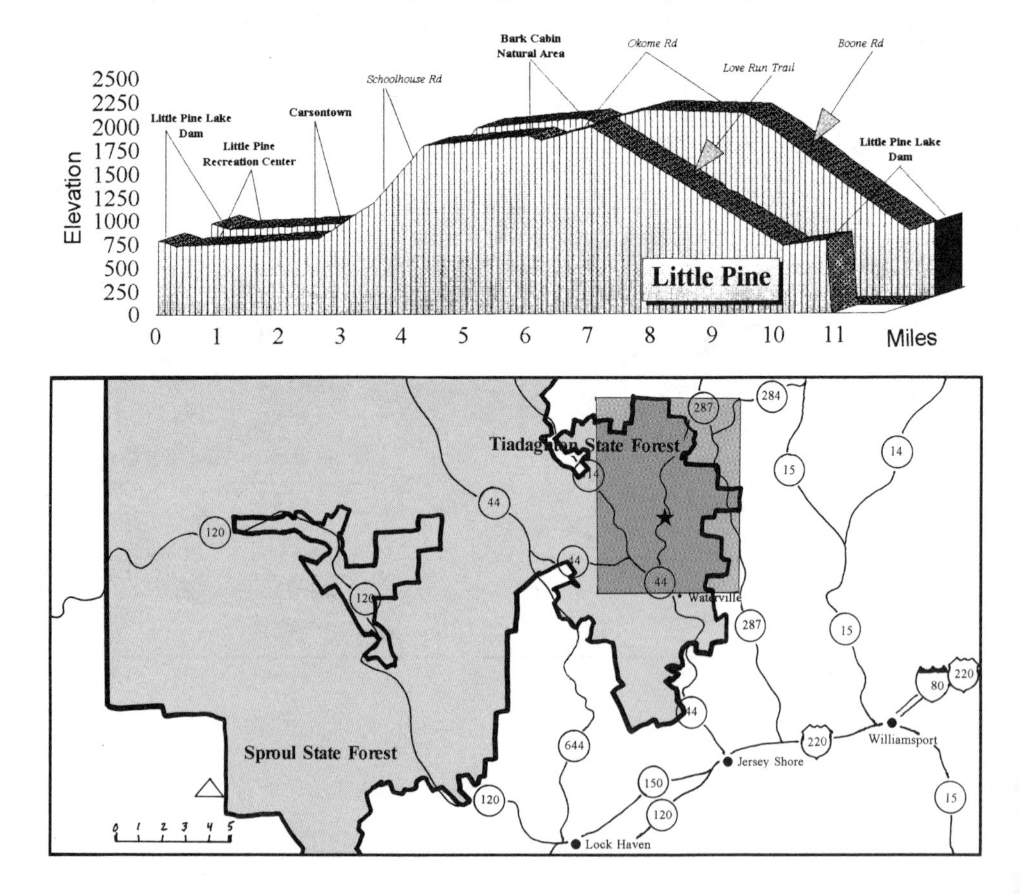

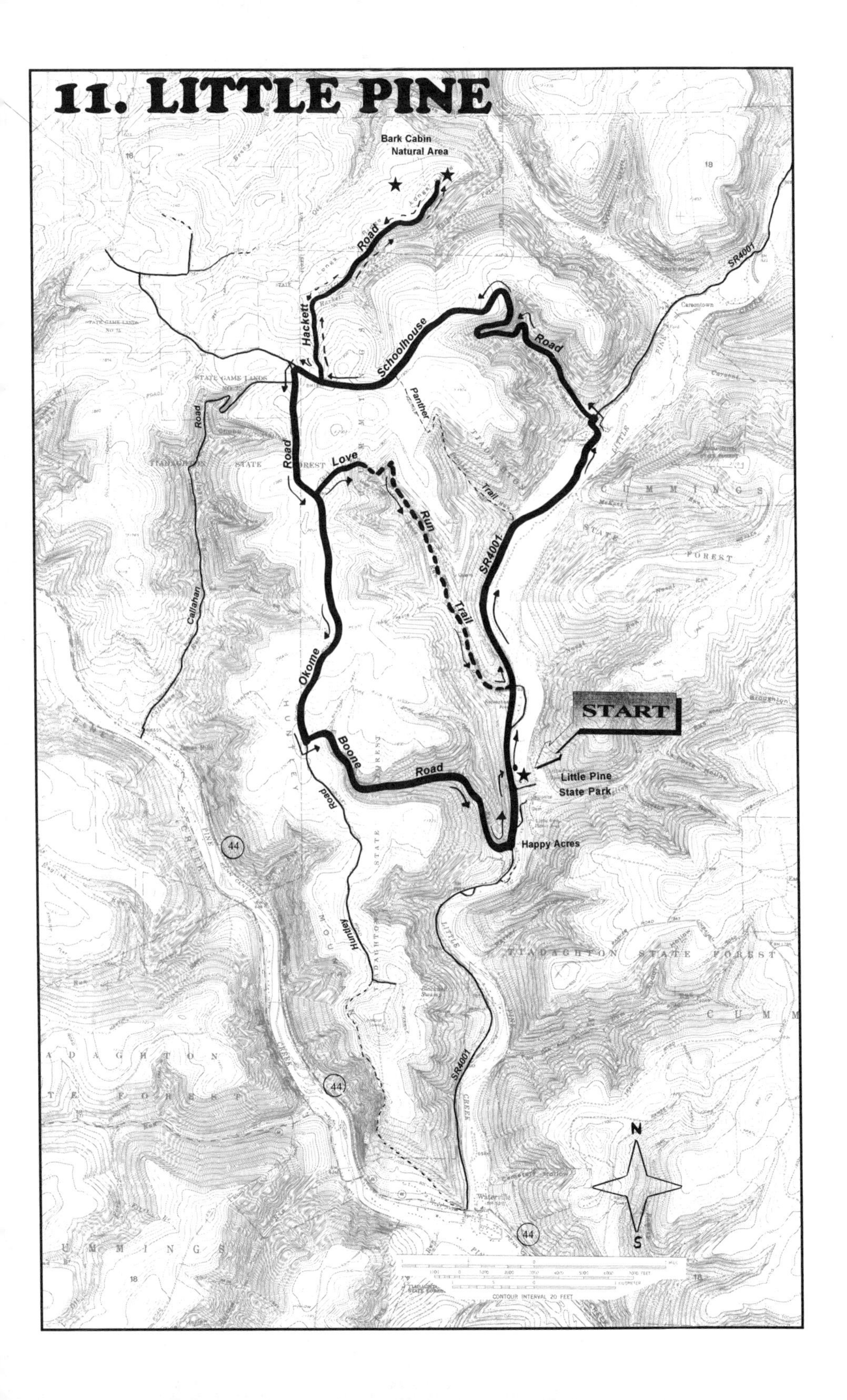
11. LITTLE PINE
Bark Cabin
Natural Area
Hackett
Road
Schoolhouse
Road
Panther
Road
Love
Run
Trail
Trail
SR4001
SR4001
Callahan
Road
Okome
Boone
Road
Road
Huntley
START
Little Pine
State Park
Happy Acres
44
44
44
SR4001
TIADAGHTON STATE FOREST
CUMMINGS
N
S
CONTOUR INTERVAL 20 FEET

Little Pine

Where To Begin ☞ *Little Pine State Park, 4 miles north of Rte. 44, 14 miles north of Jersey Shore*

MILES	DISTANCE	DIRECTIONS
0.0	0.0	**START** at the **Little Pine Lake Dam** and head north toward the recreation area and park headquarters.
0.3	0.3	**Little Pine Recreation Center:** Nature Center, Park Office, picnicking, swimming, etc. Continue north.
0.4	0.1	Pass **LOVE RUN RD** on the left. Continue north along Little Pine Creek.
2.6	2.2	Pass Carsontown cemetery on the left. Follow this road around to **SCHOOLHOUSE RD**.
2.75	0.15	Turn **left** onto **SCHOOLHOUSE RD**.
3.5	0.75	Reach the first switchback.
3.9	0.4	Reach the second switchback.
6.0	2.1	◆*Optional:* Turn **right** onto **HACKETT ROAD**. This road takes you along **Longs Ridge** toward the **Bark Cabin Natural Area**. You will have a fantastic view of **Hackett Fork** and **Bark Cabin Run Gorge** down below. Be careful though, Black Bear and an occasional rattlesnake have been spotted in this area. ★ **HACKETT ROAD** is *2.0 miles* **each** way.
6.2	0.2	After passing **HACKETT RD** turn **left** onto **OKOME RD**.

7.0	**0.8**	◆ *Your choice:*
		Turn **left** down **LOVE RUN TRAIL**. This scenic trail is lined with large hemlock trees and mountain springs. *3.1 miles* down to **Little Pine Recreation Center**. Turn **right** onto the main road. *0.7 miles* back to the dam.
		— or —
		Continue **straight** on **OKOME RD** toward **BOONE ROAD**. Lots of tall gray birch trees along this route.
9.1	2.1	Turn **left** onto **BOONE ROAD**. This great descent, surrounded by nature, follows **Boone Run** down the mountain.
11.3	2.2	Reach the bottom of the descent. Turn **left** onto Pine Hill's, **SR4001**, main road. Stop in at the **Happy Acres Restaurant** and get some serious steak for two!
11.7	0.4	Arrive back at **Little Pine Lake Dam**. Time to go for an after-ride swim.

12. PINE GORGE OVERLOOK

Start: *Waterville*	**Total Elevation Gain:** *1350 feet*
Length: *13.6 miles*	**Riding Time:** *1 hour*
Rating: *Moderate to Difficult*	**Calories Burned:** *600-1000*

This ride is bound to knock your socks off! If you survive the climb, that is. Once atop Houselander Mountain you will be treated to a view reserved only for those who want badly enough to see what eagles can see and only for those willing enough to earn it.

The ride up Dam Run is tough but scenic, then along Houselander's Plateau to a breathtaking view from the vista overlooking Pine Creek Gorge, Waterville, and much of Tiadaghton State Forest. Bring a lunch and a bottle of wine to celebrate this spot on top of the world. But don't drink too much, for the ride back down is enough of a rush in itself!

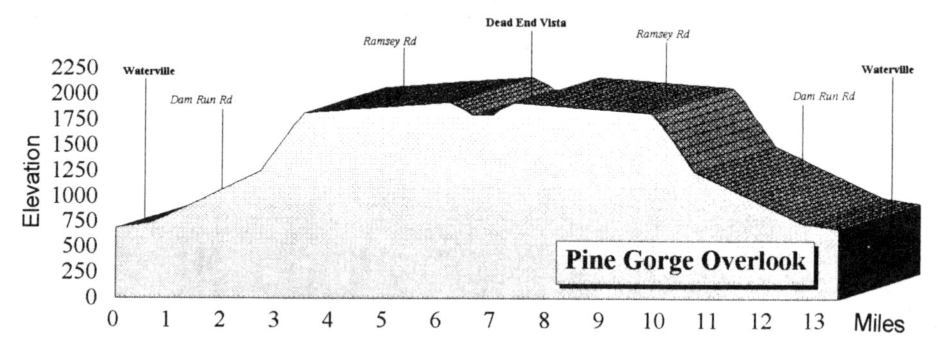

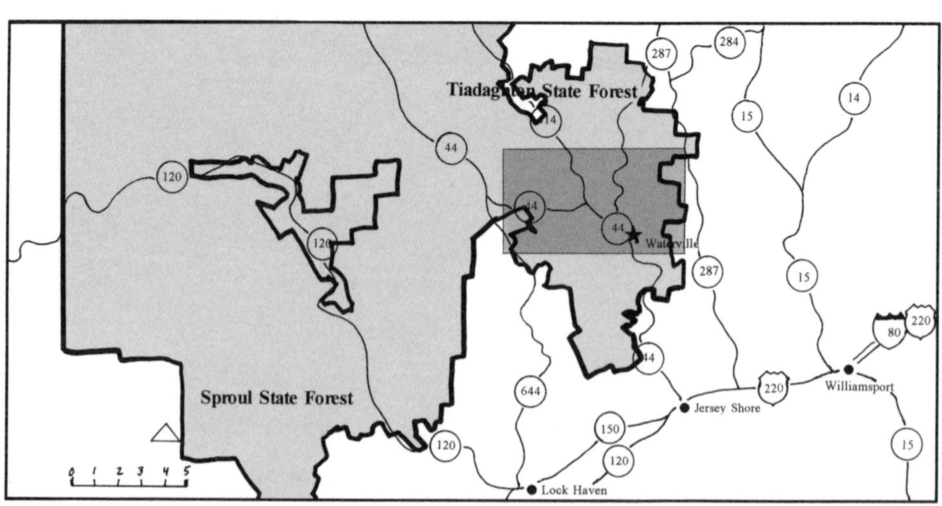

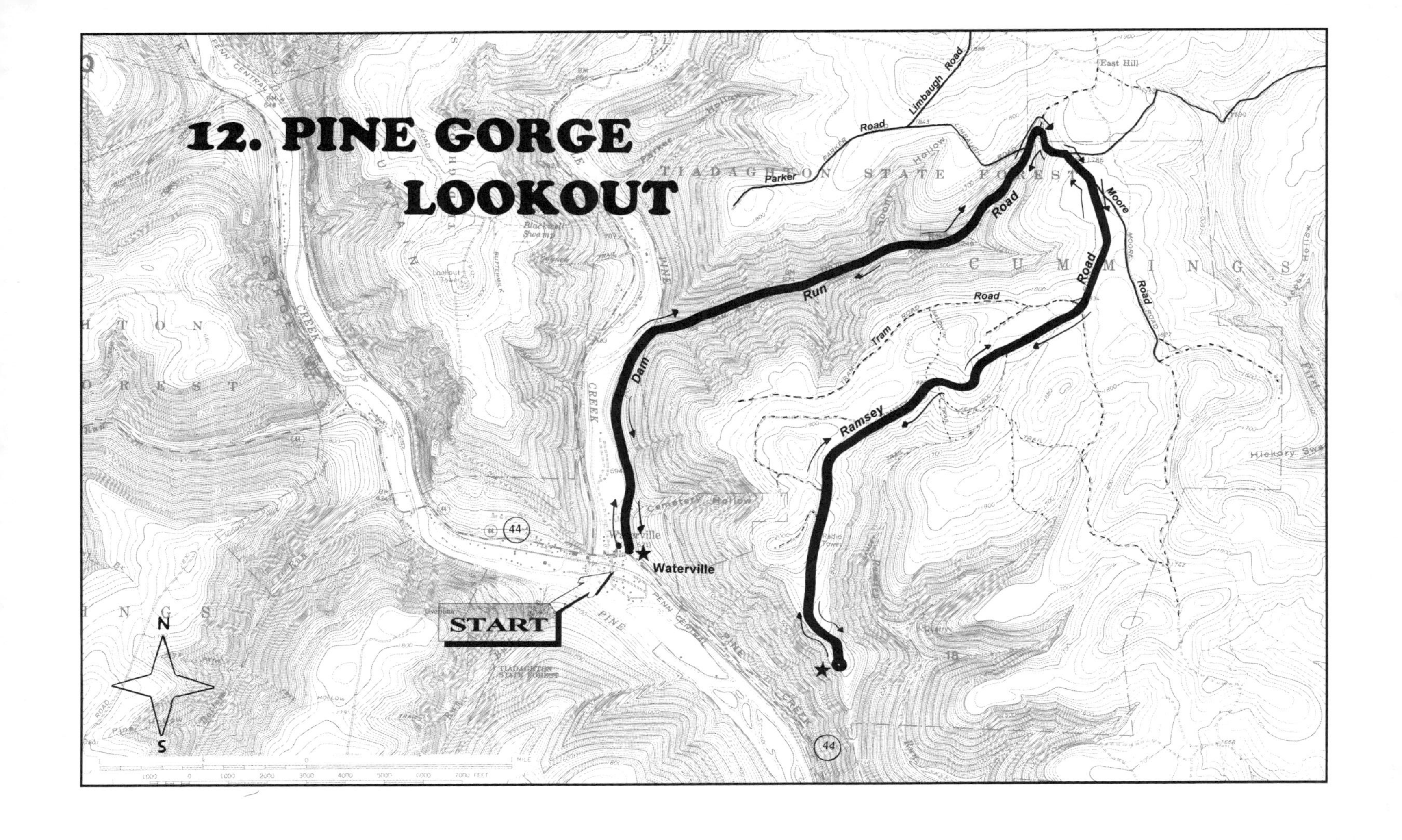
12. PINE GORGE LOOKOUT
START
Waterville
Dam Run Road
Ramsey Road
Moore Road
Parker Road
Limbaugh Road
Tram Road
East Hill
TIADAGHTON STATE FOREST
CUMMINGS
PINE CREEK
PENN CENTRAL
Cemetery Hollow
Blackwell Swamp
Radio Tower
Hickory Swamp
44
N
S
1 MILE
1000 0 1000 2000 3000 4000 5000 6000 7000 FEET

Pine Gorge Overlook

Where To Begin ☞ *Town of Waterville, just off Rte. 44, 10 miles north of Jersey Shore*

MILES	DISTANCE	DIRECTIONS
0.0	0.0	**START** in the small town of **Waterville**. Head north from **Rte 44** on **DAM RUN RD**. Start climbing. This starts out nicely paved, then deteriorates into all dirt.
0.7	0.7	**DAM RUN RD** becomes all dirt.
3.1	2.4	Bear **right** around the switchback.
3.5	0.4	Bear **right** onto **RAMSEY RD**, heading toward **Dead End Vista**.
6.2	2.7	Pass the Radio Tower on the left.
6.6	0.4	Pass a smaller vista on the right. The view is great, but just you wait.
6.8	0.2	Reach **Dead End Vista**. Look out over Pine Creek Gorge and the town of Waterville. This view should be worth the effort it took to get here. Stop and have some lunch, then turn around for a long, fun descent!
7.0	0.2	Pass vista on the left.
7.4	0.4	Radio tower on the right.
10.1	2.7	Bear **left** onto **DAM RUN RD**. Start the real descent.
10.5	0.4	Go through switchback.
12.9	2.4	**DAM RUN RD** turns to pavement.

13.6	0.7	Reach the bottom of descent at the town of **Waterville** on **Rte 44**. Hope you took some pictures. It will be tough going back up again.

13. HYNER VIEW

Start: *Hyner Run State Park*
Length: *20.2 miles*
Rating: *Moderate to Difficult*
Total Elevation Gain: *1500 feet*
Riding Time: *1½-2½ hours*
Calories Burned: *1200-2000*

This is probably one of the best rides in the book! There is something in this ride for everyone, from beautiful views of Sproul State Forest to scenic roads in the backcountry, raging singletrack descents along mountain streams, and a quiet, peaceful ride along the banks of the Susquehanna.

Bring your lunch and maybe even a camera. You may want to keep a record of this ride's many beautiful sights, including Hyner View State Park, which offers a breathtaking view of the beautiful Susquehanna River valley.

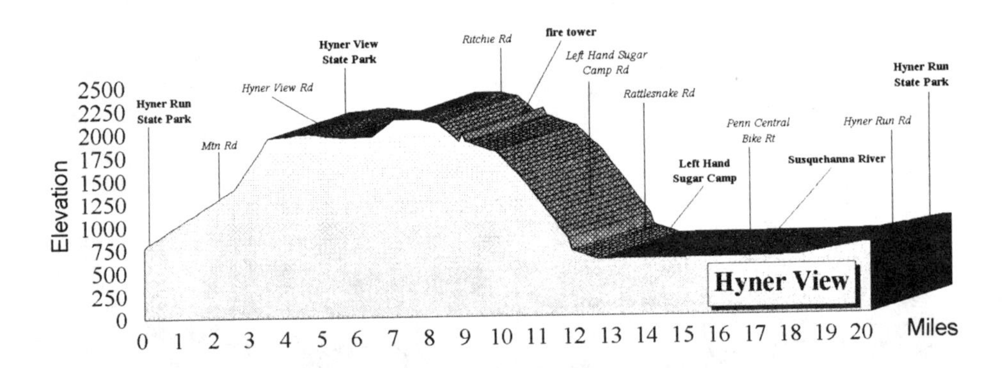

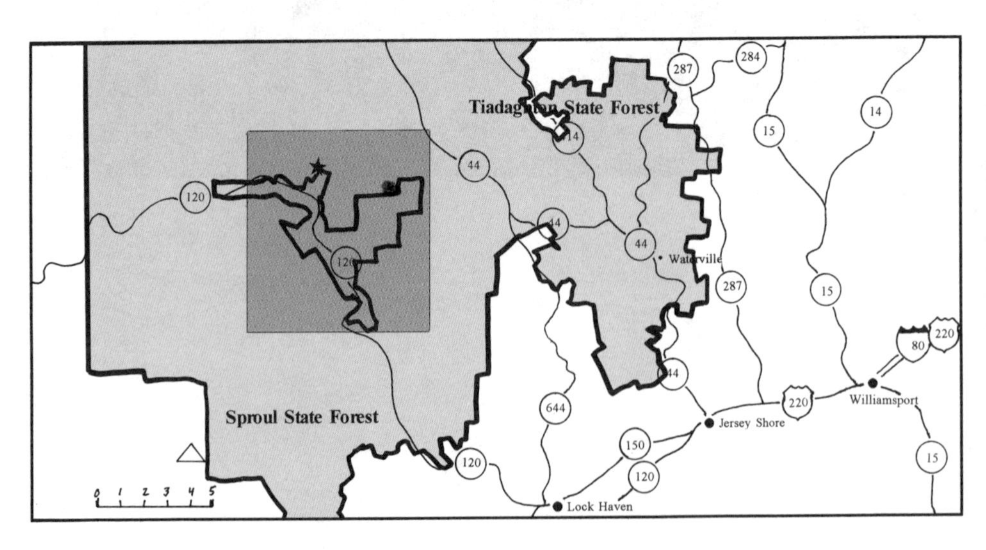

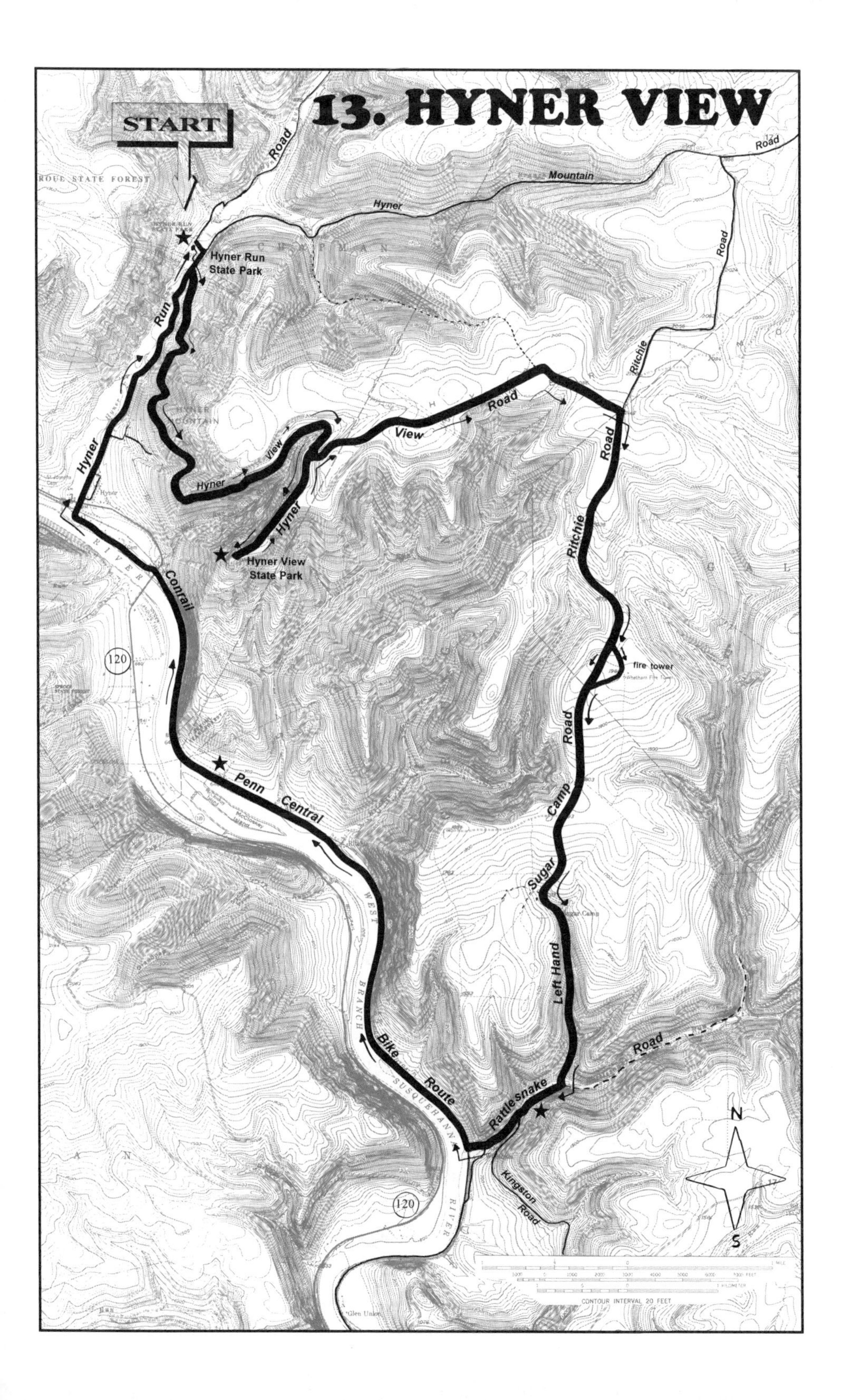

13. HYNER VIEW
START
Hyner Run State Park
Hyner View State Park
fire tower
Hyner
Run
Road
Mountain
Hyner View Road
Ritchie Road
Sugar Camp Road
Left Hand
Rattlesnake Road
Kingston Road
Contrail
Penn Central
Bike Route
120
N
S
CONTOUR INTERVAL 20 FEET

Hyner View

Where To Begin ☞ *Hyner Run State Park, just off Rte. 120, 22 miles north of Lockhaven*

MILES	DISTANCE	DIRECTIONS
0.0	0.0	**START** at **Hyner Run State Park**. Exit the campgrounds turning **right** onto **HYNER RUN RD**.
0.1	0.1	Turn **left** at the sign to **Hyner View State Park**, heading up the mountain. This is a windy, paved road.
3.5	3.4	Stay **right** on **HYNER VIEW RD**, heading toward **Hyner View**.
4.6	1.1	★ **Hyner View State Park**. The view of Sproul State Forest and the Susquehanna River below is nothing less than breathtaking. After taking in the view, turn around and head back north on **HYNER VIEW RD**.
5.7	1.1	Bear **right**, continuing on **HYNER VIEW RD** toward **RTE 44**.
6.4	0.7	Cross **pipelines**. A huge grassy swath slicing across the mountain top.
7.0	0.6	Pass Draft Hollow Trail on the left.
7.7	0.7	Turn **right** onto **RITCHIE RD**.
8.8	1.1	Stay **right** around the median or go **left** up to the fire tower. **RITCHIE RD** becomes **LEFT HAND SUGAR CAMP RD**.
9.7	0.9	Pass Dark Hollow Trail on the left. Continue on **LEFT HAND SUGAR CAMP RD**.
10.5	0.8	Bear **left** passing Twin Pine Camp. Continue descending on **LEFT HAND SUGAR CAMP RD**. This road deteriorates into an obscure, rocky jeep trail that follows the creek to the bottom of the mountain.

Hyner View

11.9	1.4	Reach the bottom. Turn **right** onto **RATTLESNAKE RD**. This follows along Rattlesnake Run.
12.2	0.3	Stay **right** on the **low** road alongside Rattlesnake Run.
		★ Left Hand Sugar Camping ground to the right on the banks of Rattlesnake Run.
12.5	0.3	Come to a big **red** and **white** tourist information center with Rattlesnake Camp written on the side. Turn **right** around this house, heading toward Rattlesnake Run.
12.55	0.05	Cross small bridge over Rattlesnake Run.
12.6	0.05	Cross **railroad tracks**, then turn **right** onto gravel road by the river. This runs along the banks of the Susquehanna River all the way to the town of Hyner.
		★ Ride along the **Susquehanna River**.
17.6	5.0	Cross underneath **RTE 120**.
18.1	0.5	Turn **right** onto **HYNER RUN RD**.
18.2	0.1	Cross **RTE 120**, heading to **Hyner Run State Park**.
20.2	2.0	Arrive at **Hyner Run State Park**. What a fantastic ride that was!

Black Moshannon State Park

Black Moshannon State Park, located in Centre County, is situated in the midst of the more than 180,000-acre Moshannon State Forest. The name Moshannon is derived from the Indian word moss-hanne, which means Moose Stream. Black Moshannon's 250-acre lake originates from crystal clear springs that flow through a number of swamps at the upper end of the lake, turning the water a dark color. It can be said that the name Black "Moose Stream" comes from this phenomenon.

Like most everything in Moshannon, Black Moshannon State Park was heavily influenced by logging. The dam, originally built by beaver, was converted to a much larger dam by a logging company to store millions of feet of timber. This timber came from the surrounding forest which, at one time, was said to be so dense with white pines that "for a mile at a time (one) could not find a place the size of a hand, where sunshine could penetrate, even in the clearest days." All of this timber was removed in the 19th and 20th centuries, leaving behind nothing but ghosts of the massive hardwoods in a time long past.

The 3,500-acre park is now covered with beech, yellow poplar, birch, maple, oak, cherry, hickory, and chestnut. In some places, there still stand tall examples of what used to be the virgin forests of white pine and hemlock.

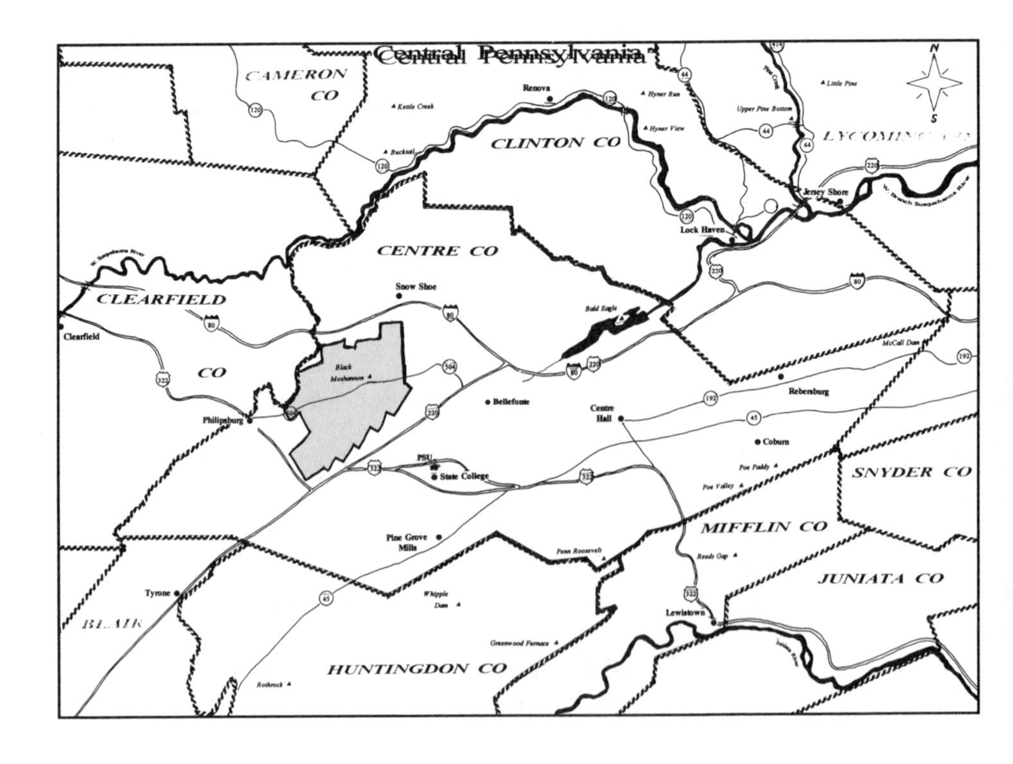

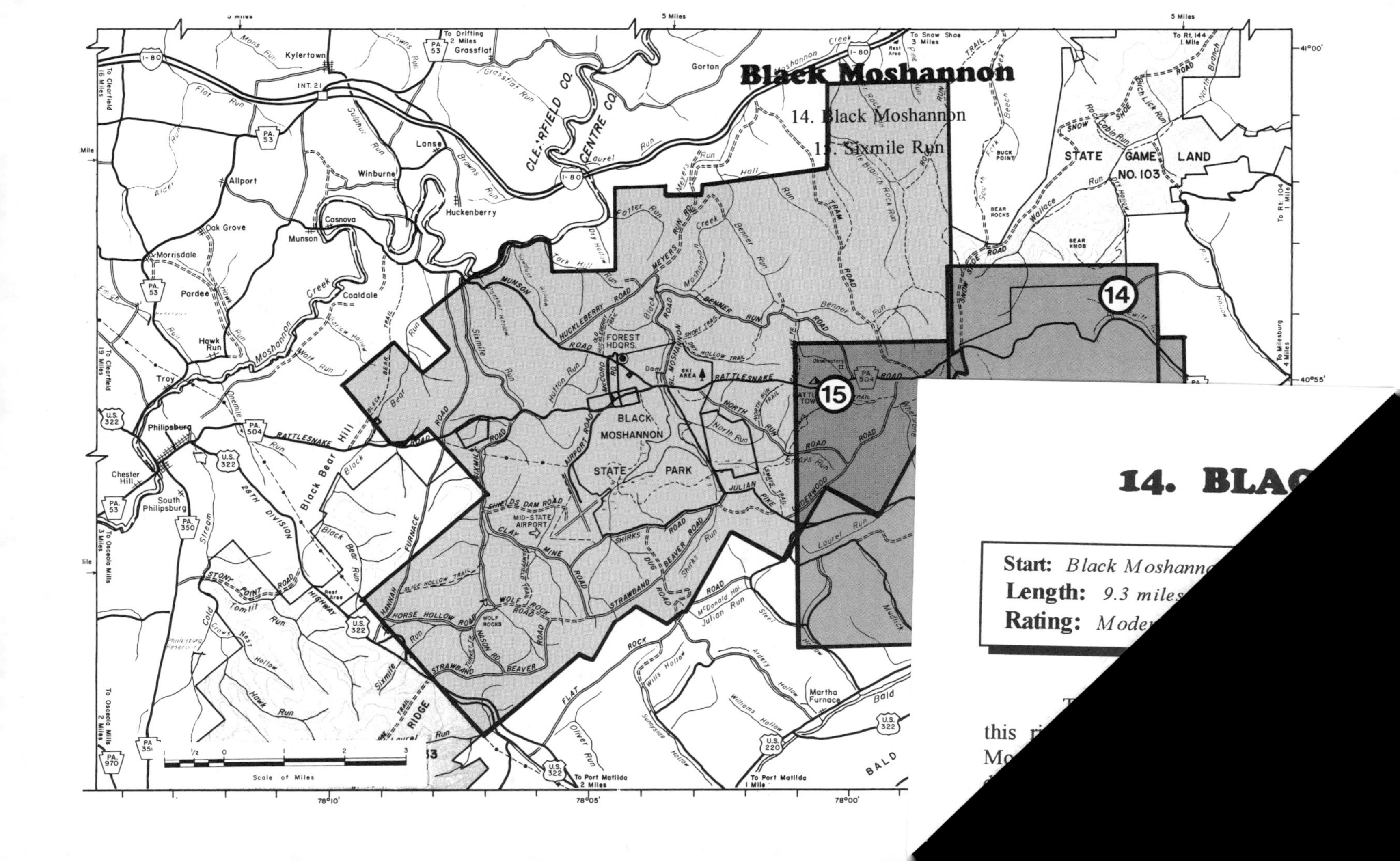
Black Moshannon
14. Black Moshannon
15. Sixmile Run
BLACK MOSHANNON STATE PARK
STATE GAME LAND NO. 103
FOREST HDQRS.
MID-STATE AIRPORT
CLEARFIELD CO.
CENTRE CO.
Philipsburg
South Philipsburg
Chester Hill
Kylertown
Grassflat
Gorton
Lanse
Winburne
Huckenberry
Casnova
Munson
Allport
Oak Grove
Morrisdale
Pardee
Coaldale
Hawk Run
Troy
Martha Furnace
To Clearfield 16 Miles
To Clearfield 19 Miles
To Osceola Mills 3 Miles
To Osceola Mills 2 Miles
To Port Matilda 2 Miles
To Port Matilda 1 Mile
To Drifting 2 Miles
To Snow Shoe 3 Miles
To Rt. 144 1 Mile
To Rt. 104 1 Mile
To Milesburg 4 Miles
Scale of Miles
14. BLAC
Start: Black Moshann
Length: 9.3 miles
Rating: Moder
this
Mo

...CK MOSHANNON

...n State Park	**Total Elevation Gain:** *640 feet*
	Riding Time: *45 minutes - 1 hour*
...ate	**Calories Burned:** *600-1000*

This is a really fun ride in a beautiful place. The 250-acre lake from which ...ide begins is fed by the State Park's many crystal clear springs. Black ...shannon is almost completely surrounded by state forest land once covered by a dense growth of pure virgin white pine and hemlock trees.

On this ride through Black Moshannon State Park you will find yourself knee-deep in a sea of fern, thickest in mid- to late summer. You may bump into a few deer and perhaps even a black bear, and find yourself flying faster down the exciting singletrack than Broad-winged Hawks in this region can fly.

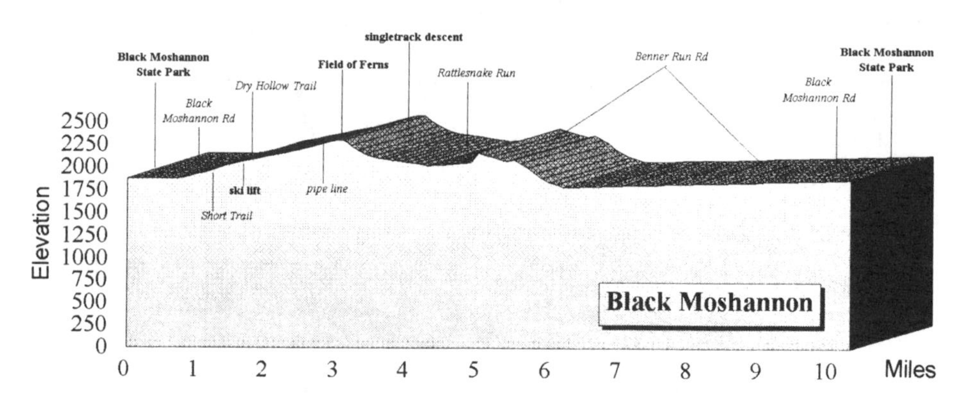

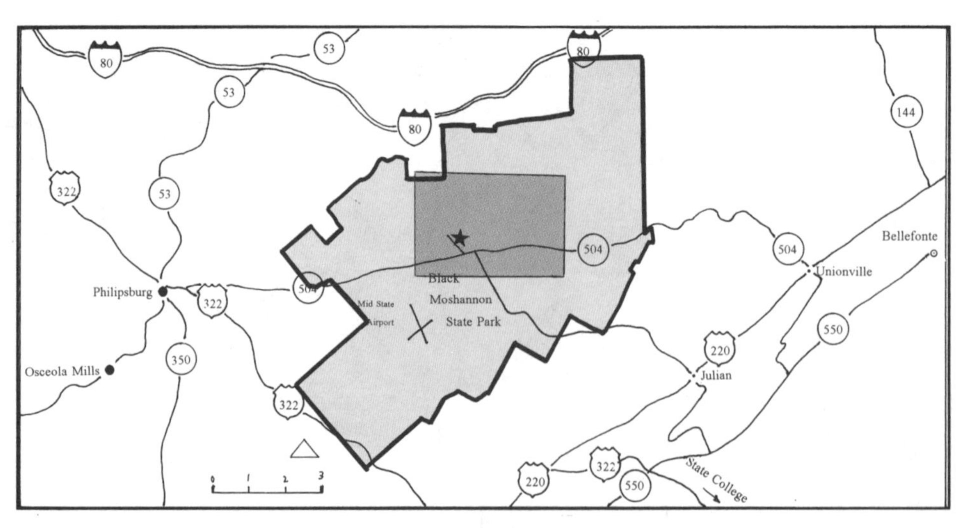

14. BLACK MOSHANNON

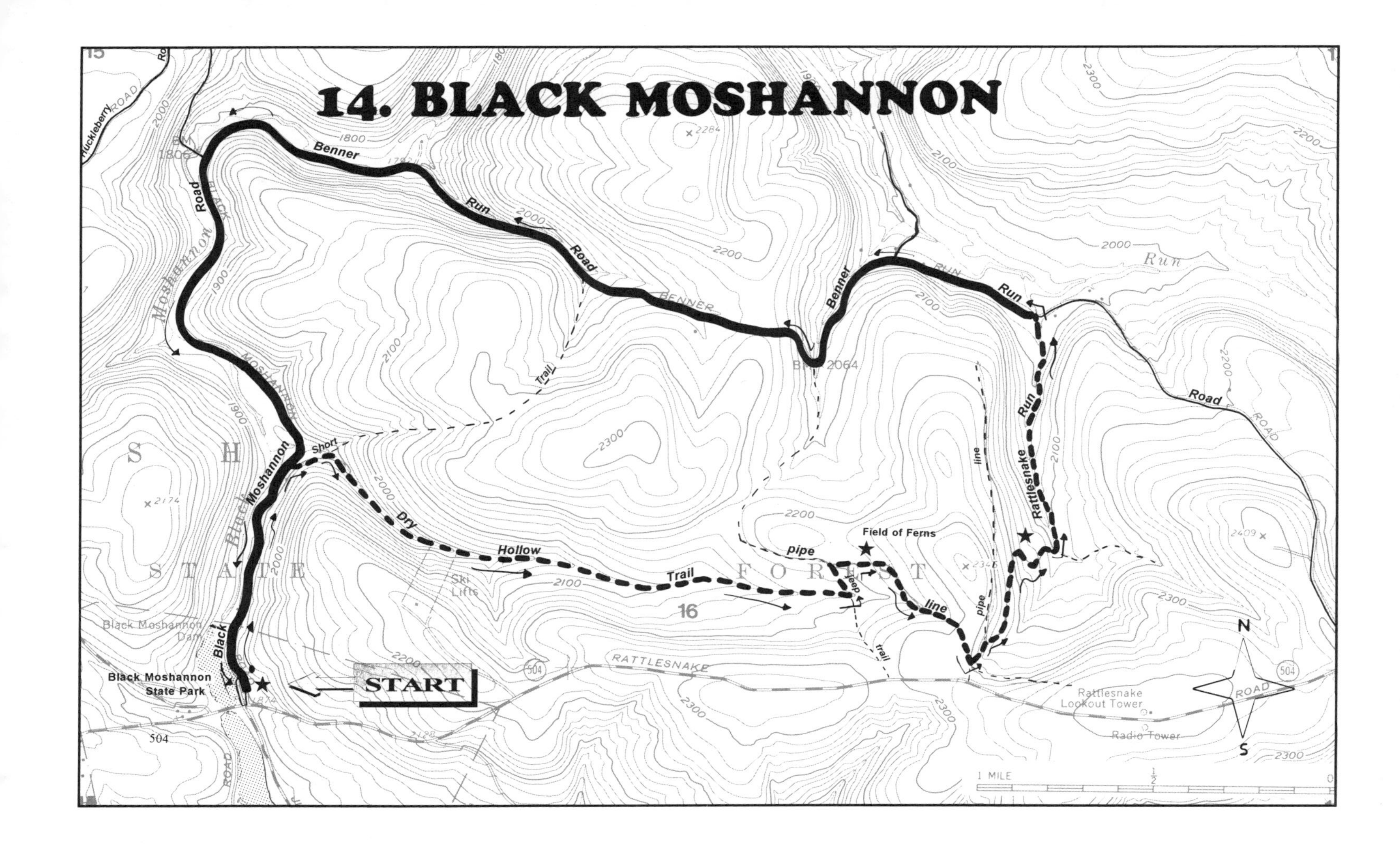

Black Moshannon

Where To Begin ☞ *Black Moshannon State Park, corner of Rte. 504 and Julian Pike, 8 miles east of Philipsburg, 18 miles north of State College*

MILES	DISTANCE	DIRECTIONS
0.0	0.0	**BEGIN** this ride from the parking lot and pedal along **BLACK MOSHANNON ROAD** into the forest.
0.2	0.2	Pass Black Moshannon Dam on the left.
0.7	0.5	On the **right** side of Black Moshannon Road, just past a small hunting lodge, is a wooden trail marker. Turn **right** here onto **SHORT TRAIL.**
0.8	0.1	The trail splits here at another wooden trail marker. **Bear right** onto **DRY HOLLOW TRAIL**.
1.2	0.4	**DRY HOLLOW TRAIL** opens up into a clearing at the base of Black Moshannon Ski Area. Continue **straight**, past the ski lifts on the right, and ride across the base of the slopes.
1.4	0.2	**Reenter** the forest, continuing on **DRY HOLLOW TRAIL**. This trail continues straight, for the most part, for a mile, ending abruptly at a grassy intersection.
2.4	1.0	At this intersection turn **left** onto the **JEEP TRAIL** and climb a quick little hill to a larger intersection of open trails.
		⋆ Be sure to notice the **orange diamonds** painted on the trees! You will follow these **orange diamonds** through some pretty crazy places and I don't want you to get lost.
2.5	0.1	★ Turn **right** at this intersection and carve your way through the "**Field of Ferns.**" The ruts on this jeep trail are nearly hidden beneath endless rows of knee-high ferns.
2.9	0.4	Start up a short, steep climb.

3.1	0.2	A bit past the top of this hill, turn **left** onto the **JEEP TRAIL** and start a quick descent.
		★ Watch for the moguls as you zip downhill. You can catch some good air. Keep your eyes peeled for a quick **right-hand**. It comes up quick!
3.2	0.1	Bear **down** and to the **right**, turning off this jeep trail and onto a **singletrack trail** that cuts across the mountain side, overlooking the valley. This drops off suddenly, then snakes its way into the forest below.
		★ You will see more **orange diamond** markers along the way. Beware of the hidden moguls on the fast, twisting descent. Too bad there's no lift, so we can race down over and over again.
3.6	0.4	Reach the bottom of the descent. Turn **left** onto **RATTLESNAKE TRAIL**. Follow the **orange diamonds** along this rocky, flat trail.
4.3	0.7	**Exit RATTLESNAKE TRAIL** through the trees and turn **left** onto **BENNER ROAD**.
7.5	3.2	At the crossroads of **Benner Rd, Huckleberry Rd, and Black Moshannon Rd**, bear **left** and follow **BLACK MOSHANNON ROAD** back towards the park. This is a nice place to rest and watch Black Moshannon Creek from the bridge.
9.3	1.8	**Arrive** at Black Moshannon Park and race over to the car, being sure to skid through the parking lot throwing gravel in every direction. Watch the paint on those cars though!

15. SIXMILE RUN

Start: *Black Moshannon State Park*
Length: *14.2 miles*
Rating: *Easy to Moderate*
Total Elevation Gain: *300 feet*
Riding Time: *1-1½ hours*
Calories Burned: *600-1000*

This ride starts off with a meandering ride along Sixmile Run. It then takes you along quiet forest roads through Black Moshannon's scenic outdoors and rolling beauty.

For the seasonal color watchers out there, this ride is for you. The fall colors along this route are absolutely spectacular and very easy to enjoy. The roads you'll be travelling move along slowly through Black Moshannon State Park. You won't be rushed, and the ambers, orange, reds, and gold may even have you off your bike not moving at all. Just stop and enjoy because few places in autumn are as beautiful.

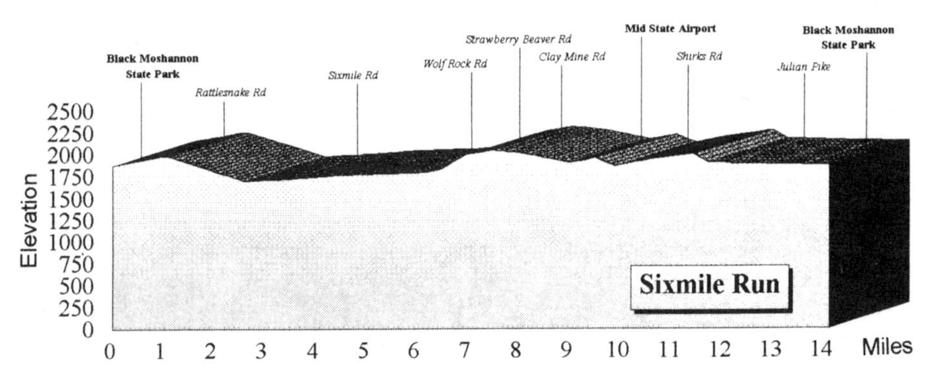

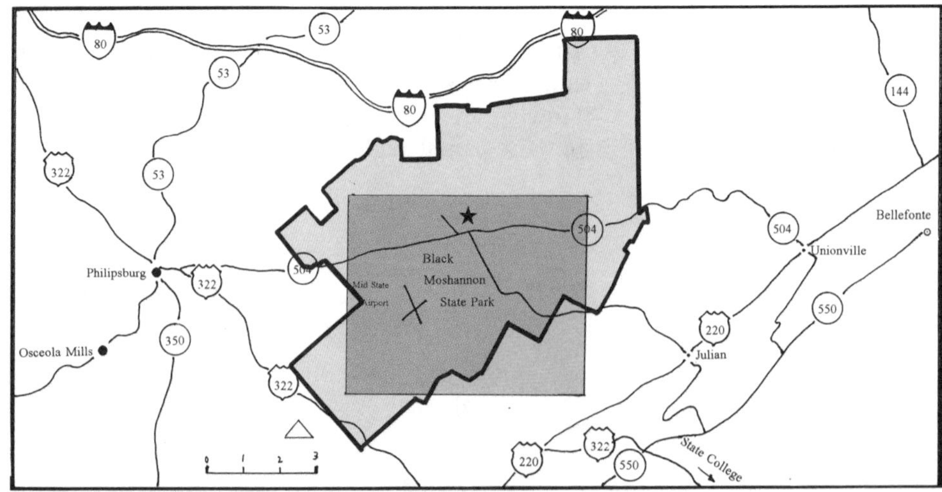

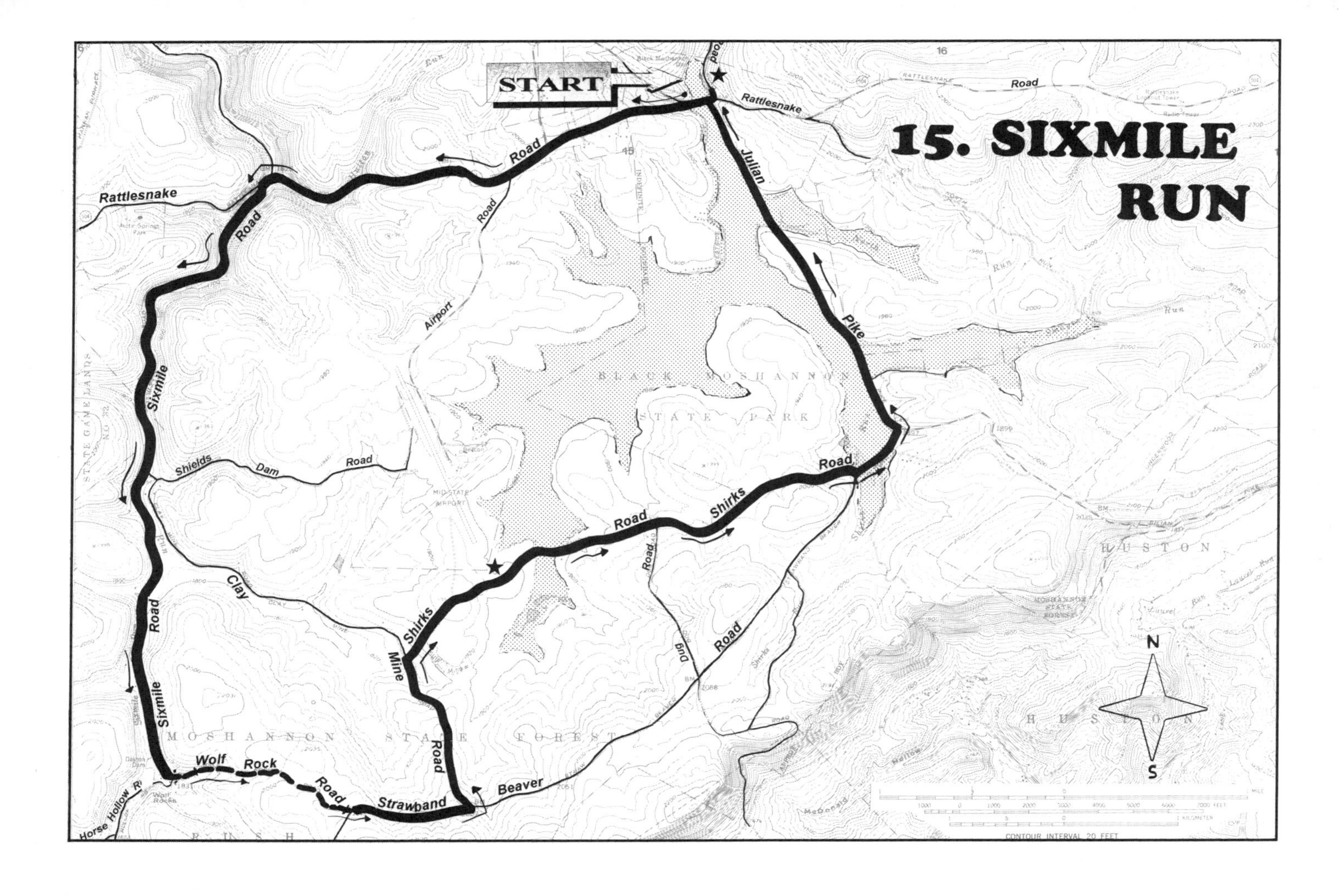
15. SIXMILE RUN
START
Road
Rattlesnake
Rattlesnake
Road
Julian
Pike
Road
Airport
Road
Sixmile
Shields
Dam
Road
Shirks
Road
Shirks
Road
Clay
Mine
Road
Dug
Road
Road
Sixmile
Wolf
Rock
Road
Strawband
Beaver
Horse Hollow R
BLACK MOSHANNON STATE PARK
MOSHANNON STATE FOREST
HUSTON
N
S
CONTOUR INTERVAL 20 FEET

Sixmile Run

Where To Begin ☞ *Black Moshannon State Park, corner of Rte. 504 and Julian Pike, 8 miles east of Philipsburg, 18 miles north of State College.*

MILES	DISTANCE	DIRECTIONS
0.0	0.0	**START** at **Black Moshannon State Park**. Head **west** on **RTE 504, RATTLESNAKE RD**. Cross bridge over the lake.
1.1	1.1	Pass **Airport Rd** on the left. Continue on **RATTLESNAKE RD**.
2.6	1.5	Cross the bridge over Sixmile Run and turn **left** onto **SIXMILE RUN RD**. The creek will be below on your left.
4.5	1.9	Pass **Shields Dam Rd** on the left. Continue on **SIXMILE RUN RD**.
6.2	1.7	Pass Dayton Dam on the right.
6.4	0.2	Enter the small camping village of Wolf Rocks. Turn hard **left** between two green and white buildings onto **WOLF ROCK RD**. You will have to go around the gate onto this grassy jeep trail.
7.5	1.1	Turn **left** onto **STRAWBAND BEAVER RD**.
8.1	0.6	Turn hard **left** at trail markers onto **CLAY MINE RD**.
9.0	0.9	Turn **right** onto **SHIRKS RD**.
9.6	0.5	★ Pass **Mid State Airport** on the left.
10.0	0.4	Cross over the **Black Moshannon Marsh**.
10.6	0.6	At the trail intersection, continue **straight** on **SHIRKS RD**.
11.8	1.2	Turn **left**, continuing toward **Julian Pike**.

12.1	0.3	Turn **left** onto **JULIAN PIKE**, heading back towards **Black Moshannon** and the beach,the food, and some rest.
14.2	2.1	Reach Black Moshannon State Park.

Some Other Great Places

16. The Barrens

Once a small mining region set up by Andrew Carnegie in the late 19th century, Scotia has since closed its furnaces and sold its land to the Pennsylvania Game Commission for public recreation. This area is under a grouse habitat management program studying the behaviors of the State bird. Ironically, the area's shooting range is also in Scotia, but the two are not in conflict. Deer, grouse, and other small game all thrive in this gently rolling, lush environment just a few miles west of State College.

17. Toftrees/Deer Pens

This town is not only home to Penn State University's 35,000 students and the world famous Nittany Lions, it's also smack dab in the middle of the state! Mountain biking on the east coast got its start here in State College, a town surrounded by state forests. Mountain biking is king in this college town, and Happy Valley is happy to welcome cyclists to its trails.

There are a number of bike routes around town, including the old abandoned railroad bed which makes for some perfect off-road cycling

18. Wilderness 101

This ride starts in the small town of Coburn and travels through Bald Eagle State Forest into Rothrock State Forest, then back again. It takes you through virtually every park and picnic area from Poe Paddy to Whipple Dam. This course is based on the famous *Wilderness 101* bike race. Once a year hundreds of mountain bike racers from around the country travel to Central PA to test their strengths against the country's longest single-lap, one-day, off-road race.

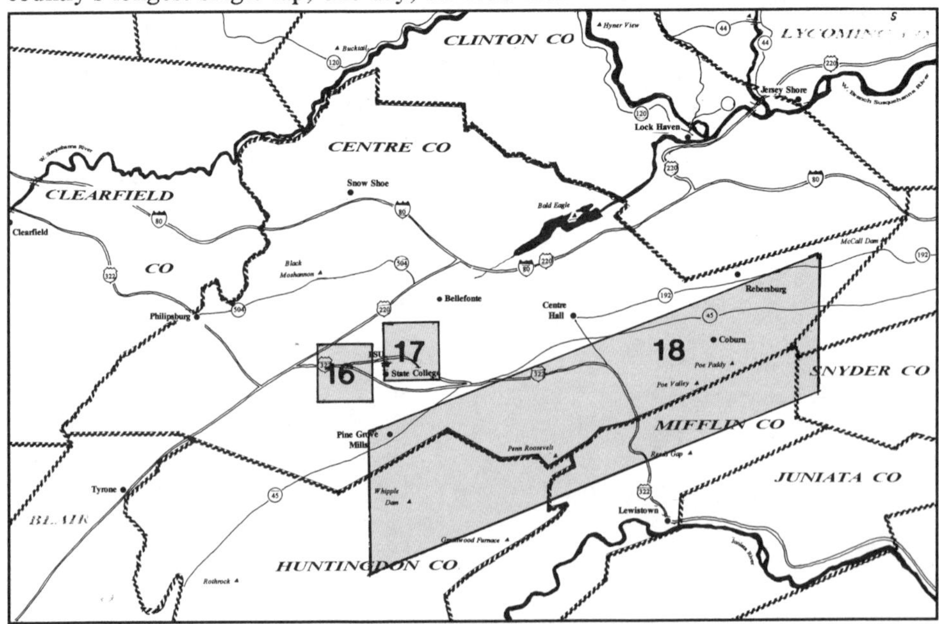

Through Moshannon's forest

16. THE BARRENS

Start: *Scotia Target Range*	**Total Elevation:** *200 feet*
Length: *4.3 miles*	**Riding Time:** *30-45 minutes*
Rating: *Easy*	**Calories Burned:** *400-600*

Here's a fun ride that rolls along the grassy trails of Scotia Range through what is called The Barrens. Many of these trails are marked in quadrants for the grouse habitat program. Park Officials are studying the effects of habitat management on grouse populations.

Through the grassy feed line you are almost guaranteed to see dozens of deer grazing in the clearing. A look is about all you'll get though, as the white tails disperse quickly into the trees. Exploring other trails in this area is also highly recommended. Scotia Range and The Barrens are fantastic places for a great mountain bike.

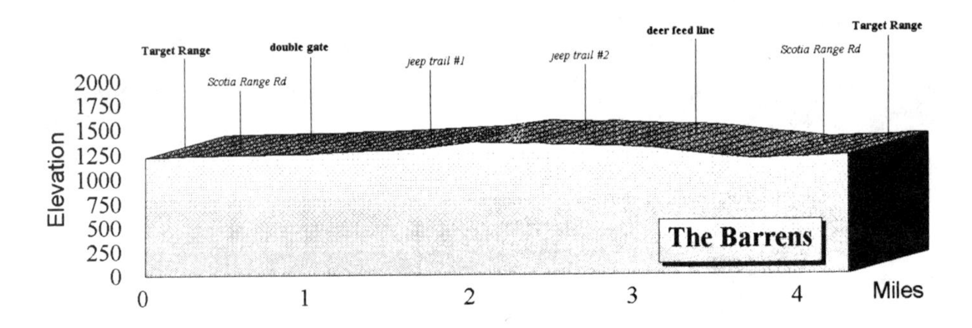

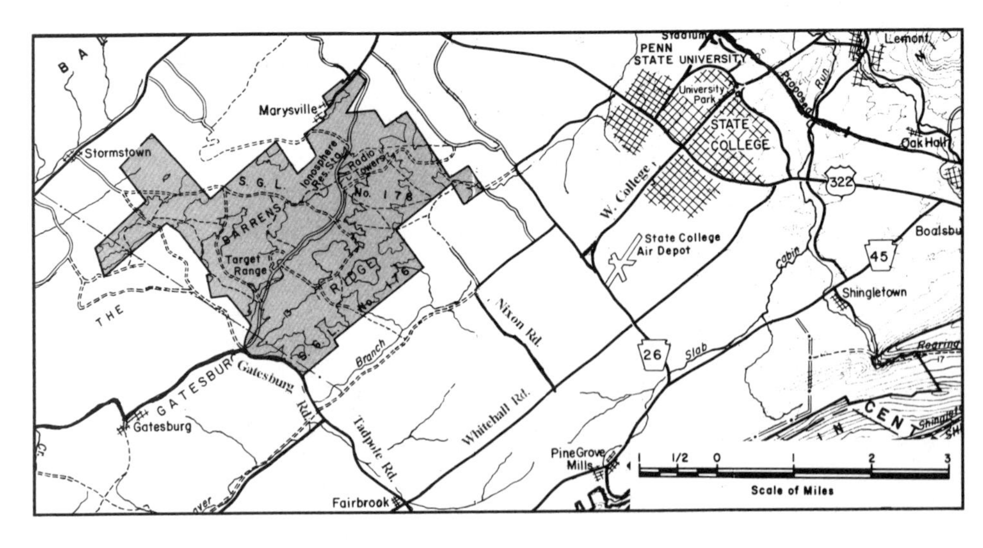

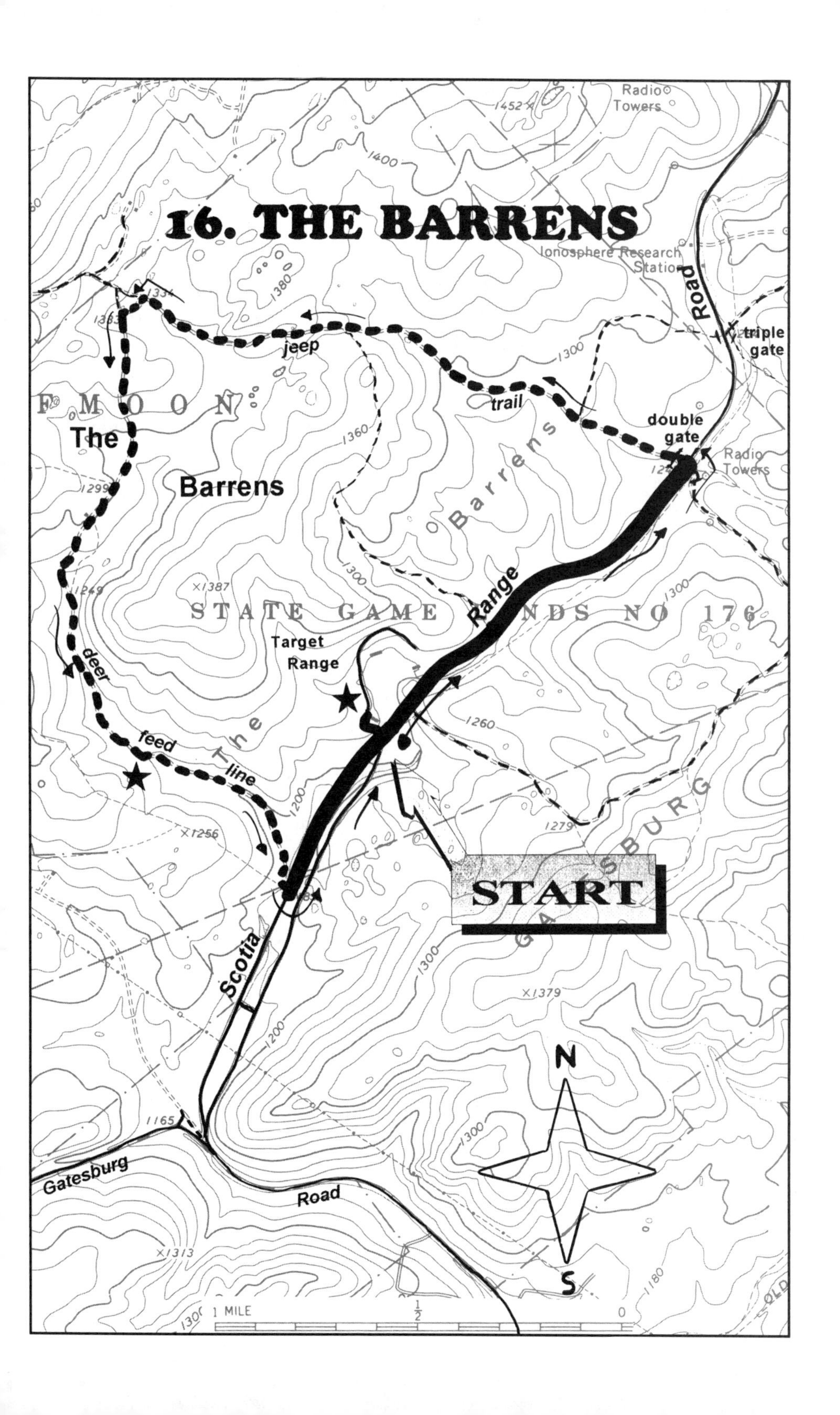

16. THE BARRENS
Radio Towers
Ionosphere Research Station
Road
triple gate
jeep
trail
double gate
Radio Towers
The
Barrens
The Barrens
Range
STATE GAME LANDS NO 176
Target Range
deer
feed
line
START
Scotia
GATESBURG
N
S
Gatesburg
Road
1 MILE
½
0

The Barrens

Where To Begin ☞ *Scotia Target Range, 1 mile east of Gatesburg, 2 miles west of Rte 322, approximately 8 miles east of State College*

MILES	DISTANCE	DIRECTIONS
0.0	0.0	**START** at the parking lot at **Scotia Range**. Exiting the parking area and target range turn **left** onto **SCOTIA RD**.
1.0	1.0	Turn **left** onto a large grassy swath clearing on both the left and right of the road. There are **double gates** here.
2.0	1.0	Come to a small clearing. Continue **straight**, passing a grassy trail on the left. This trail takes you back to Scotia Rd.
2.0	0.5	Turn **left** at this intersection. Follow this **JEEP TRAIL** as it descends into the woods.
2.6	0.1	Stay **left**, continuing on the grass **JEEP TRAIL**.
3.1	0.6	Enter a long open grassy feed section. This trailway leads you all the way down to Scotia Rd. ★ This feed line brings dozens of deer and other wildlife into the clearing. Especially near dusk, deer practically crowd into this area.
3.7	0.6	Turn **left** onto **SCOTIA RD**.
4.3	0.6	Arrive back at **Scotia Range**. Watch out for flying bullets at the firing range!

17. TOFTREES/DEER PENS

Start: *Penn State's Flower Garden*	**Total Elevation Gain:** *T: 300 feet; D: 385 feet*
Length: *T: 5.7 miles; D: 4.1 miles*	**Riding Time:** *T: 30 mins.; D: 30 mins.*
Rating: *T: Easy; D: Easy*	**Calories Burned:** *300-500*

Here's a pair of rides for Penn State students in need of a serious study break. Alumni are welcome, of course, but please, no blue and white outfits! Just north of Penn State's campus, these rides are easy to get to and fun for riders of all levels of ability.

The first of these two rides takes you along the old rail bed to Toftrees Resort and its 18-hole PGA championship golf course. While you're in the area, try out their hike and bike routes, fitness trail, horse-drawn carriage rides, great food, and more.

The second of these rides gives you a quick taste of some simple singletrack before taking you up to the Deer Research Center, where you can watch live deer at only an arm's length away.

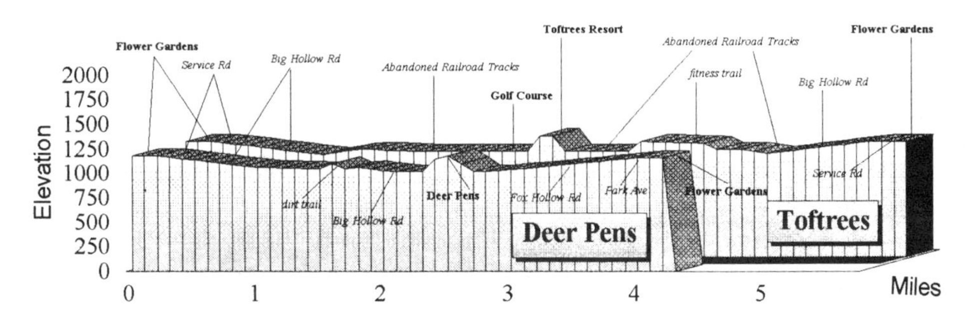

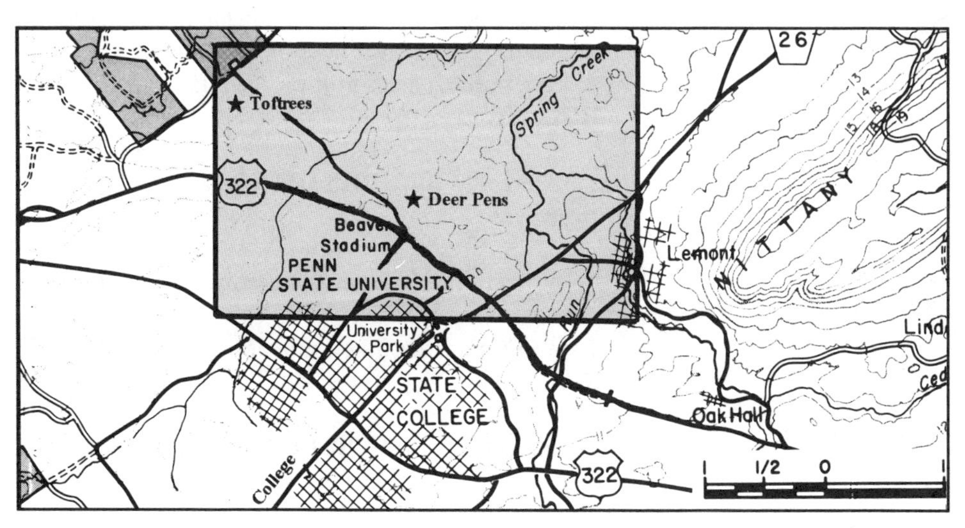

Deer Pens

Where To Begin ☞ *Penn State's flower gardens at the corner of Park Ave and Bigler Rd, across from East Halls, 2 miles north of State College*

MILES	DISTANCE	DIRECTIONS
0.0	0.0	**START** at Penn State's **Flower Gardens** on the north end of campus. Follow **SERVICES RD,** heading north, away from campus.
0.1	0.1	**Hard right** around the bend. Pass Food Services Building on the left.
0.2	0.1	Turn **left** onto **BIG HOLLOW RD**, taking you away from the playing fields.
1.0	0.8	Just after the hard right bend at the bottom of the hill turn **left** off of **BIG HOLLOW RD** onto the **gravel road**. Burned firefighter test building is on the right.
1.05	0.05	Continue **straight** at the fork on this gravel road heading into the woods.
1.5	0.45	This gravel road ends at a large electrical utility box. Turn **right** onto a small **trail** at the end of this road. The trail heads up into the woods along side a fence. Follow this **trail** through the woods.
1.7	0.2	Exit the woods after a quick downhill, continuing on this **trail**. Arrive at a large power station. Pass the power station and follow the trail up to **BIG HOLLOW RD**.
1.8	0.1	Turn **left** onto **BIG HOLLOW RD** heading toward the **Deer Pens**.
1.9	0.1	Come upon the gate across the road. Go around it.
2.1	0.2	Turn **left** onto the **bike route** along **FOX HOLLOW RD**.
2.2	0.1	Turn **right** onto **BIG HOLLOW RD**. This changes back to a gravel road.

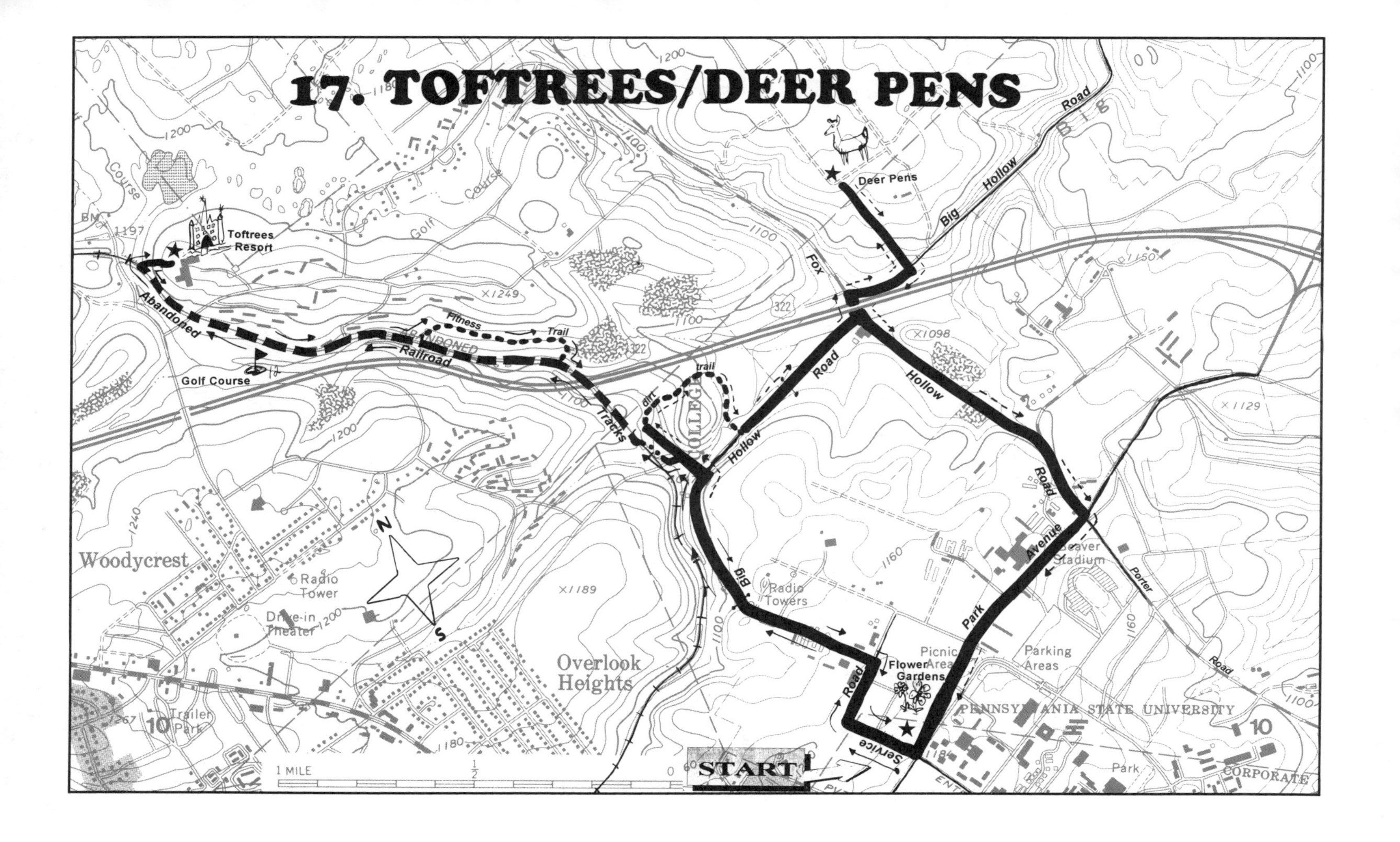

17. TOFTREES/DEER PENS
Deer Pens
Big Hollow Road
Toftrees Resort
Golf Course
Course
Abandoned Railroad Tracks
Fitness Trail
dirt trail
Fox Hollow Road
COLLEGE
322
Big Hollow Road
Park Avenue
Beaver Stadium
Porter Road
Radio Towers
Picnic Area
Flower Gardens
Parking Areas
PENNSYLVANIA STATE UNIVERSITY
Service Road
START
Woodycrest
Radio Tower
Drive-in Theater
Overlook Heights
Trailer Park
Park
CORPORATE
N
S
1 MILE
1/2
0

2.3	0.1	Turn **left** to the **Deer Research Center**. Short uphill.
2.5	0.2	★ Arrive at the **Deer Pens**. Look at the pretty deer. **Return**.
2.7	0.2	Turn **right** onto **BIG HOLLOW RD**.
2.8	0.1	Turn **left** onto the **bike route** along **FOX HOLLOW RD**.
3.7	0.9	Turn **right** at the stop light onto **PARK AVE**. Pass Penn State's **Beaver Stadium** on the left.
3.9	0.2	Cross **UNIVERSITY DR** at the stop light, continuing on **PARK AVE**. Pass **East Halls** on the left.
4.1	0.2	Turn **right** onto **SERVICES RD**. Arrive at Penn State's **Flower Gardens**. I imagine the flowers smell better than those deer.

Toftrees

Where To Begin ☞ *Penn State's flower gardens at the corner of Park Ave and Bigler Rd across from East Halls, 2 miles north of State College.*

MILES	DISTANCE	DIRECTIONS
0.0	0.0	**START** at Penn State's **Flower Gardens** on the north end of campus. Follow **SERVICES RD,** heading north, away from campus.
0.1	0.1	**Hard right** around the bend. Pass Food Services Building on the left.
0.2	0.1	Turn **left** onto **BIG HOLLOW RD**, taking you away from the playing fields.
1.0	0.8	Just after the hard right bend at the bottom of the hill turn **left** off of **BIG HOLLOW RD** onto the **gravel road**. Burned firefighter test building is on the right.
1.05	0.05	Bear **left** at the fork. Head up toward the farmland.
1.1	0.05	Turn **right** off the road onto the dirt trail before you pass through the gates to the farmland. This trail takes you up to the old railroad bed.
1.2	0.1	Merge onto the **ABANDONED RAILROAD TRACKS**, staying north.
1.4	0.2	Cross underneath **RTE 322**.
2.2	0.8	Arrive at Toftrees' golf course, hole #12.
2.5	0.3	Cross **Toftrees Avenue**. Continue straight on the dirt trail along side of the golf course.
2.7	0.2	Turn hard **right** up the steep hill to **Toftrees Resort**. This turn comes just before the trail crosses a wooden trestle over the golf course. It brings you out at the tennis courts.

2.75	0.05	★ Arrive at **Toftrees Resort**. Check out their food, tennis, championship golf, lake, and more.
		« NOTE » Toftrees requests that bikes **do not** ride on their paved paths around the golf course. Please walk your bikes around the resort area if you wish to explore the beautiful grounds.
2.8	0.05	Ride back down to the **ABANDONED RAILROAD TRACKS** and turn **left**, heading back toward State College.
		If you were to go right and follow the abandoned railroad bed, it would take you toward Bellefonte. However, the trail disappears in the weeds near Rte 550. There are plans to turn this into a "rails to trails" route from Bellefonte to State College sometime in the future.
3.0	0.2	Cross **Toftrees Avenue**. Continue on dirt trail along the golf course.
3.3	0.3	Pass hole #12.
3.5	0.2	Bear **left** onto **FITNESS TRAIL-Leg Stretch #8**. This goes up the hill into the woods.
3.6	0.1	Reach the top of the climb. This is a short, steep, rough climb. Enjoy! Follow the **FITNESS TRAIL** through the woods.
3.8	0.2	Cross an open section for the sewer system. Continue on this **through-the-woods** trail.
4.1	0.3	Exit the woods into a large open area. Follow the trail to the **right**. It should lead you back into the woods and downhill to the railroad bed.
4.15	0.05	Turn **left** on the **ABANDONED RAILROAD TRACKS**, heading back toward Penn State.
4.5	0.35	Reach the gravel road where you entered onto this trail. Ride to **BIG HOLLOW RD**.

4.6	0.1	Turn **right** onto **BIG HOLLOW RD** going uphill back to the **Flower Gardens**.
5.3	0.7	Reach the top of the climb.
5.4	0.1	Turn **right** onto **SERVICES RD**. Penn State's playing fields are on the left.
5.7	0.3	Arrive back at the Penn State's **Flower Gardens**. Who says there's not enough time to stop and smell the roses?

MOTORIZED
VEHICLES
PROHIBITED

18. WILDERNESS 101

Start: *Coburn Schoolhouse*	**Total Elevation Gain:** *6815 feet*
Length: *101.8 miles*	**Riding Time:** *8-10 hours*
Rating: *Difficult*	**Calories Burnes:** *6400-8000*

Not only is this the longest ride in the book , but also the longest single-lap off-road route in the country. This ride is a slightly modified version of the original *Wilderness 101* bike race, now an annual event in Central Pennsylvania for which hundreds of racers from around the nation arrive to compete. The modifications in this book are made primarily to avoid confusing sections of the original course and to direct overnighters to Greenwood Furnace State Park's camping ground. For the most part, however, this route is virtually identical, just as brutal, and every bit as awesome as the original *101.*

You will start in Bald Eagle State Forest and work your way southwest over mountains, through parks, and past stunning overlooks into Rothrock State Park. Nearly all points of interest are covered along this long route, including Alan Seeger, Whipple Dam, Big Flat, Bear Meadows, Poe Paddy, railroad tunnels, trestles, and more. Bring along some camping gear, spend a few days on the backroads, and have a great weekend of riding.

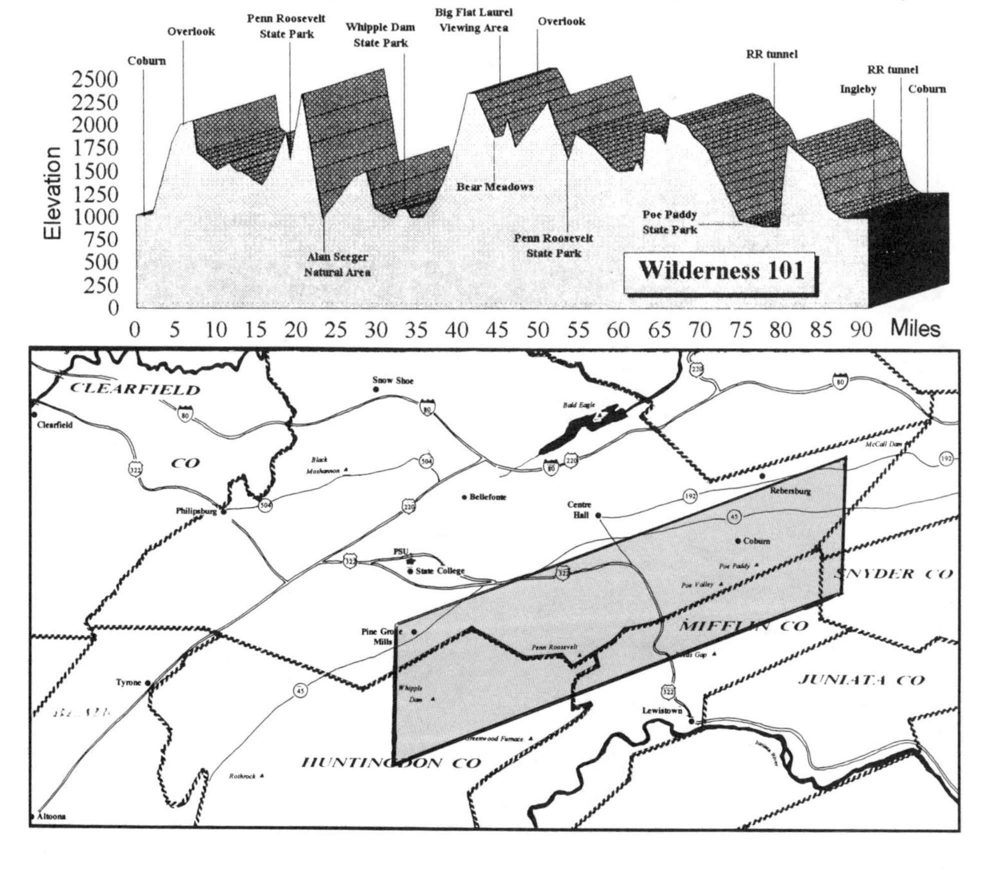

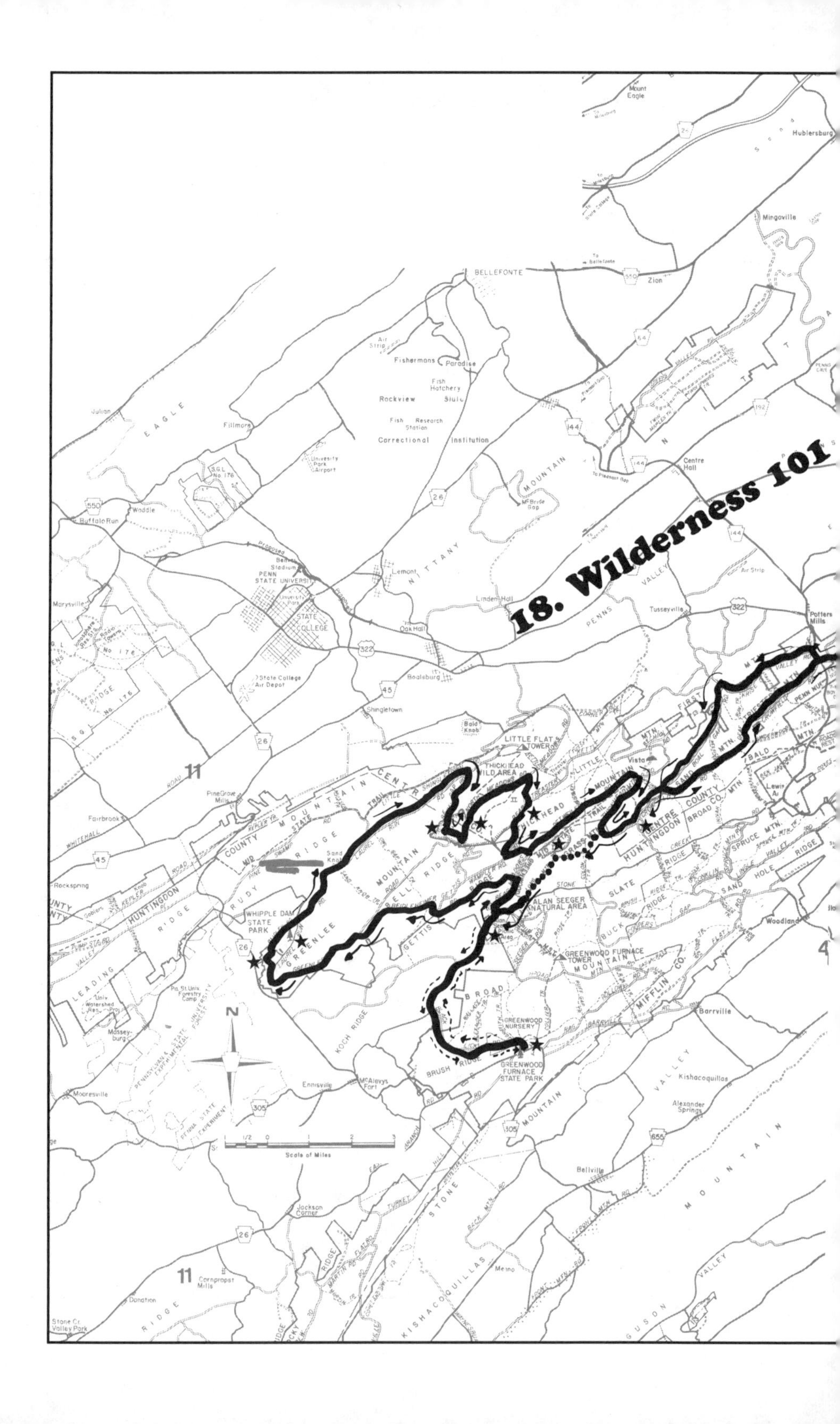
18. Wilderness 101
Mount Eagle
Hublersburg
Mingoville
BELLEFONTE
Zion
Fishermans
Paradise
Fish Hatchery
Rockview
Fish Research Station
Correctional
Institution
Julian
Fillmore
EAGLE
University Park Airport
S.G.L. No. 176
Waddle
Buffalo Run
MOUNTAIN
McBride Gap
Centre Hall
NITTANY
Lemont
PENN STATE UNIVERSITY
STATE COLLEGE
Linden Hall
Oak Hall
PENNS VALLEY
Tussey ville
Potters Mills
Air Strip
Boalsburg
State College Air Depot
Marysville
Shingletown
Bald Knob
LITTLE FLAT TOWER
THICKHEAD WILD AREA
Vista
Pine Grove Mills
Fairbrook
Sand Knob
WHIPPLE DAM STATE PARK
GREENLEE
Rockspring
HUNTINGDON
ALAN SEEGER NATURAL AREA
GREENWOOD FURNACE TOWER
Woodland
HUNTINGDON BROAD CO.
CENTRE COUNTY
MIFFLIN CO.
Barrville
BROAD
GREENWOOD NURSERY
GREENWOOD FURNACE STATE PARK
KOCH RIDGE
BRUSH RIDGE
Pa. St. Univ. Forestry Camp
Univ. Watershed
Masseyburg
N
Ennisville
McAlevys Fort
Mooresville
Kishacoquillas
Alexander Springs
Scale of Miles
STONE
Bellville
Jackson Corner
Cornpropst Mills
Donation
Stone Cr. Valley Park
Meno
KISHACOQUILLAS

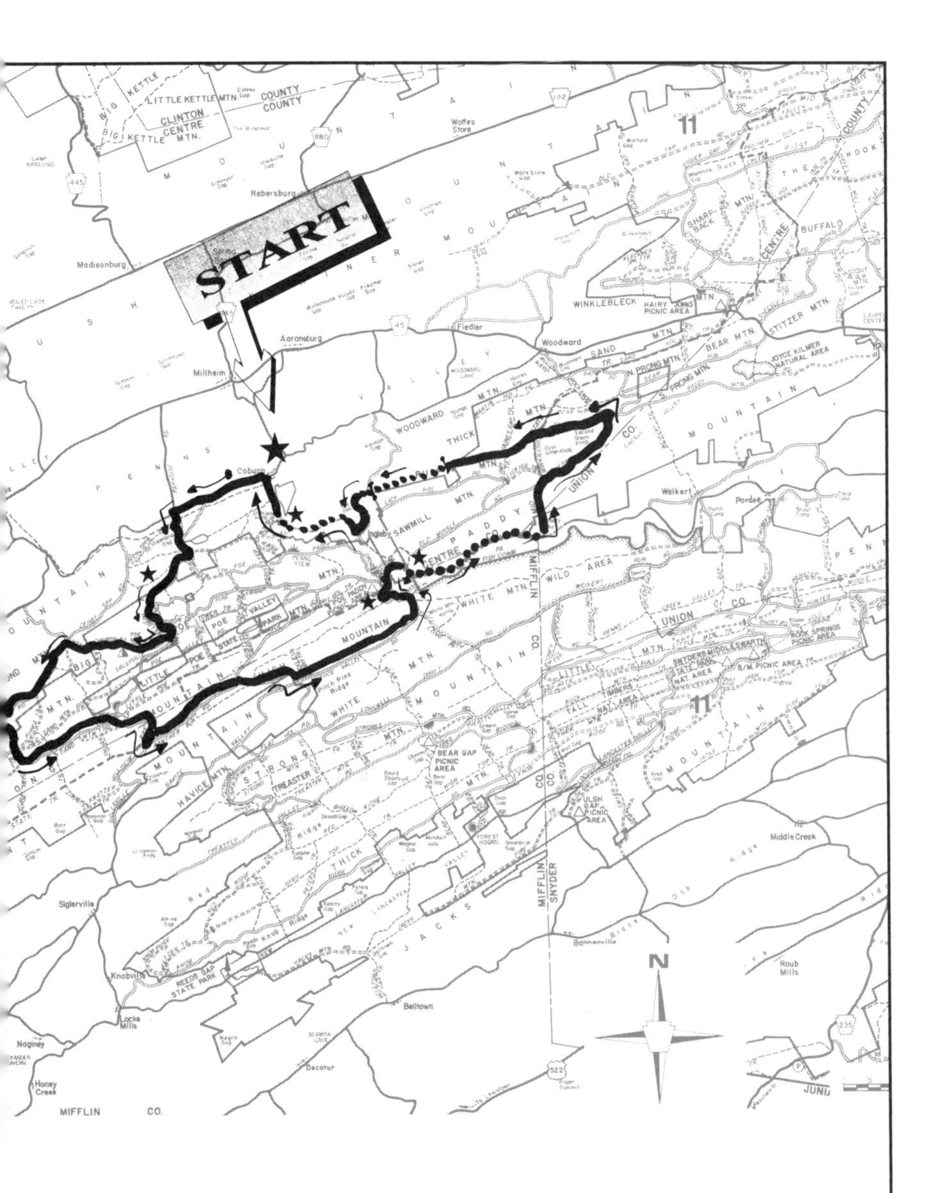

Note: The **Wilderness 101** is raced annually, sponsored by community organizations. To learn more about this event, please contact your local bike and outdoor stores.

Wilderness 101

Where To Begin ☞ *Town of Coburn, south of Rte. 45, 18 miles east of State College, just below Millheim*

MILES	DISTANCE	DIRECTIONS
0.0	0.0	**START** at the **Penn Township School** parking lot. Turn **left** onto **GEORGES VALLEY RD (Main St)**.
0.1	0.1	Bear **right** at the bridge, continuing on **GEORGES VALLEY RD**.
2.0	1.9	Turn **left** onto **MILLHEIM PIKE**, crossing the bridge over Penns Creek.
4.4	2.2	★ Scenic vista on the right.
4.6	0.2	Pass **Pine Swamp Rd** on the left.
5.5	0.9	Reach the summit. Turn **right** onto **CHURCH RD**.
7.7	2.2	At this intersection turn **left** onto **DECKER VALLEY RD**.
9.8	2.1	At this intersection crossing **Synagogue Rd**, go **straight**, continuing on **DECKER VALLEY RD**.
12.6	2.8	Turn **right** onto **RTE 322**. Be ready to turn left back into the woods. Watch traffic!
12.9	0.3	Turn **left** onto **KRISE VALLEY RD**. Look both ways before crossing this highway! This is at a **red mailbox** just before the restaurant up the road. Cross a small bridge as you reenter the forest.
15.4	2.5	Arrive at Boal Gap. Turn **left** onto **BOAL GAP RD**. Start climbing.
16.4	1.0	Bear **left** over a small bridge, continuing on **BOAL GAP RD**.
18.4	2.0	Reach the top of the climb. Stay **right** onto **CROWFIELD RD.**

19.2	0.8	Reach the bottom of the climb.
		★ Penn Roosevelt State Park. Relax at the small lake.
		Take the first possible **right** turn onto **THICKHEAD MOUNTAIN RD**. This is an uphill, rocky **jeep trail**.
19.5	0.3	Go around the steel gate. Continue up **THICKHEAD MOUNTAIN RD**.
20.1	0.6	Turn **left** off of **Thickhead Mtn Rd** onto **LONG MOUNTAIN TRAIL**. Keep your eyes open for this! You should notice on the left a very small clear spot on the side of **Thickhead Mtn Rd** that leads into a thin mountain trail up the mountain. This trail is marked by a tree and a wooden post with a ribbon wrapped around it. Follow this trail over the mountain. It turns into a larger **jeep trail** over the top of the mountain.
20.5	0.4	Reach the summit of Grass Mountain. **Long Mountain Trail** becomes more prominent at this point. Start descending the long descent to Alan Seeger.
22.8	2.3	Turn **right** onto **STONE CREEK RD**. This paved road takes you to **Alan Seeger Natural Area**.
23.1	0.3	Turn **right** at the clearing and cross a small bridge heading into **Alan Seeger Natural Area**.
		★ **Alan Seeger Natural Area**.
		« NOTE »
23.6	0.5	**For overnighters**... Turn left onto **BLACK LICK RD** toward **Greenwood Furnace State Park**. You will find plenty of camping available here. 5.8 miles to **Greenwood Furnace Park**. The next day, return 5.8 miles on **BLACK LICK RD** back to this point and continue with the next cue.
		★ **Overnighters**, follow the **bold MILES** column to the end of the ride. If you did not stay overnight at Greenwood Furnace, and are doing this ride in one

			day, continue following the unbold MILES column.
35.2	23.6	0.5	Turn **right** off pavement onto **BEAR MEADOWS RD**.
36.3	24.7	1.1	Turn **hard left** onto **BEIDLEHEIMER RD**. Climb over Gettis and Bell Ridge.
38.5	26.9	2.2	Pass **Gettis Ridge Rd**. Continue on **BEIDLEHEIMER RD**.
41.0	29.4	2.5	Turn **left** onto **GREENLEE RD**. Head toward **Whipple Dam State Park**.
43.4	31.8	2.4	**GREENLEE RD** ends at the pavement. Turn **right** onto **LAUREL RUN RD**.
43.8	32.2	0.4	Turn **left** onto **WHIPPLE DAM RD**.
43.9	32.3	0.1	★ Arrive at **Whipple Dam State Park**. Stop and relax! Go for a swim, eat a lunch, or just hang out at this beautiful park.
			Continue on **WHIPPLE DAM RD**, heading toward the **Northwest Shore**. Cross the bridge over the water falls.
44.0	32.4	0.1	Turn **left** toward the Park's exit.
44.2	32.6	0.2	Turn **right** after the wooden median onto **BEIDLER RD**.
			★ This road takes you through a tunnel of white pines in the **Laurel Run Natural Area**.
45.5	33.9	1.3	Turn **left** onto **LAUREL RUN RD**. Start climbing.
47.4	35.8	1.9	Pass Sand Knob on the left.
48.4	36.8	1.0	Go **Straight** at the intersection with **Pine Swamp Rd.** Continue on **LAUREL RUN RD**.
48.6	37.0	0.2	Pass Owl Gap Lodge on the right.

51.1	39.5	2.5	Turn hard **right** onto **BEAR GAP RD**. Still climbing!
52.4	40.8	1.3	Reach the summit!
52.7	41.1	0.3	Turn **left** onto **GETTIS RIDGE RD**.
			★ **Big Flat Laurel Viewing Area** near this intersection.
53.4	41.8	0.7	Turn hard **left** onto **NORTH MEADOWS RD**.
54.0	42.4	0.6	★ Scenic vista on the right overlooking **Bear Meadows**. Start the descent.
56.4	44.8	2.4	Turn hard **right** onto **BEAR MEADOWS RD**.
57.0	45.4	0.6	★ **Bear Meadows National Landmark**. Start climbing.
57.6	46.0	0.6	Reach the summit of **Thickhead Mountain**. Start a quick descent.
58.5	46.9	0.9	Turn hard **left** onto **WAMPLER RD**.
59.2	47.6	0.7	Turn **left** onto **DETWEILER RD**.
62.7	51.1	3.5	Turn **right** onto **THICKHEAD MOUNTAIN RD**. Start a fast descent down to Penn Roosevelt State Park.
65.3	53.7	2.6	★ **Penn Roosevelt State Park**.
			Stay **left**, continuing up **CROWFIELD RD**. Start climbing.
66.2	54.6	0.9	Bear **right** passing **Boal Gap Rd**. Continue on **CROWFIELD RD**.
71.2	59.6	5.0	Cross **RTE 322** to **DECKER VALLEY RD**. Enter **DECKER VALLEY RD** at the large brown sign reading "Penn Nursery and Wood Shop. Bureau of Forestry"
71.3	59.7	0.1	Pass Wolf's Used Car & Garage on the right. Mtn. Acres on the left.

An abandoned railroad tunnel

73.9	62.3	2.6	Turn **right** onto **SYNAGOGUE RD**. Start climbing.
74.7	63.1	0.8	Reach the top of the climb. Stay **left** at this intersection, following the sign for Poe Valley State Park. Start descending.
75.6	64.0	0.9	Pass **Summit Trail**.
76.6	65.0	1.0	Pass **Indian Trail**.
77.1	65.5	0.5	Turn **hard right** onto **MILLHEIM PIKE**.
78.5	66.9	1.4	Turn hard **left** onto **PANTHER RUN RD**. Start descending.
80.8	69.2	2.3	Turn **right** onto **LITTLE POE RD**.
82.0	70.4	1.2	Turn **left** onto **HAVICE VALLEY RD**.
85.4	73.8	3.4	Penns Creek on the right.
86.1	74.5	0.7	★ After the hairpin turn, turn **right** at the main entrance into **Poe Paddy State Park**. Follow the sign pointing toward "Coburn 11 miles."
86.15	74.55	0.05	Cross over the little wooden bridge. Stay **RIGHT** at this intersection. Do **not** follow the sign toward Coburn.
86.7	75.1	0.55	Turn **right** at **Ramsey Rd** (3 houses to the left). **Mid State Trail.** This is the **Abandoned Railroad bed**.
86.8	75.2	0.1	Cross Penns Creek over the wooden railroad trestle.
86.85	75.25	0.05	★ Go through the tunnel. Be careful, it's dark in there!
			Follow the old rail bed to **Cherry Run Rd**.
89.4	77.8	2.55	Come to a gate. Bear **right** off the rail bed down onto a dirt road.
89.8	78.2	0.4	Turn **left** onto **CHERRY RUN RD**. This goes underneath the abandoned railroad.

90.8	79.2	1.0	Bear **right**, continuing on **CHERRY RUN RD**.
92.4	80.8	1.6	Turn **left** onto **RUPP HOLLOW RD.**
95.6	84.0	3.2	Go through the gate, continuing on **RUPP HOLLOW RD**, now a jeep trail.
97.1	85.5	1.5	Go through this gate. Turn **left** onto **INGLEBY RD**.

« NOTE »

To stay with the actual ***101*** course, turn **left** onto **LICK HOLLOW RD**. Follow this around to **OLD MINGLE RD** and turn **right**. At the end of **OLD MINGLE RD** there is a distinct "fisherman's path" singletrack along the river. This connects with the **abandoned railroad** and takes you into **Ingleby**. Approximately 6.5 miles. Continue at this point with the following directions.

98.8	87.2	1.7	Enter **Ingleby**. At road's end, turn **right** onto the abandoned railroad. This is a dark graveled path.
			★ Be sure to notice the **Ingleby Rock** hanging from a tripod in the "village square." This rock is claimed to have mythical Indian powers.
100.2	88.6	1.4	Cross railroad trestle over Penns Creek.
100.3	88.7	0.1	★ Go through the tunnel.
101.1	89.5	0.8	Get onto the dirt road parallel to the railroad bed.
101.4	89.8	0.3	Turn **right** toward Penns Creek. Follow this road into the town of Coburn.
101.7	90.1	0.3	Cross bridge into Coburn.
101.8	90.2	0.1	Arrive at Penn Township School! Congratulations! You have just completed the longest single-lap course in the country!

APPENDIX

APPENDIX A

REPAIR AND MAINTAIN

FIXING A FLAT

TOOLS YOU WILL NEED

- Two tire irons
- Pump (either a floor pump or a frame pump)
- **Not a screwdriver!!!** (This can puncture the tube)

REMOVING THE WHEEL

The front wheel is easy. Simply open the quick release mechanism or undo the bolts with the proper sized wrench, then remove the wheel from the bike.

The rear wheel is a little more tricky. Before you loosen the wheel from the frame, shift the chain into the smallest gear on the freewheel (the cluster of gears in the back). Once you've done this, removing and installing the wheel, like the front, is much easier.

REMOVING THE TIRE

STEP ONE: Insert a tire iron under the bead of the tire and pry the tire over the lip of the rim.

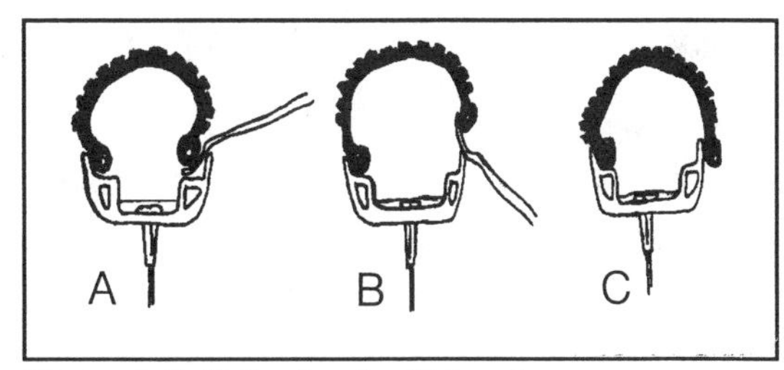

Figure 1 Pull the bead off the rim

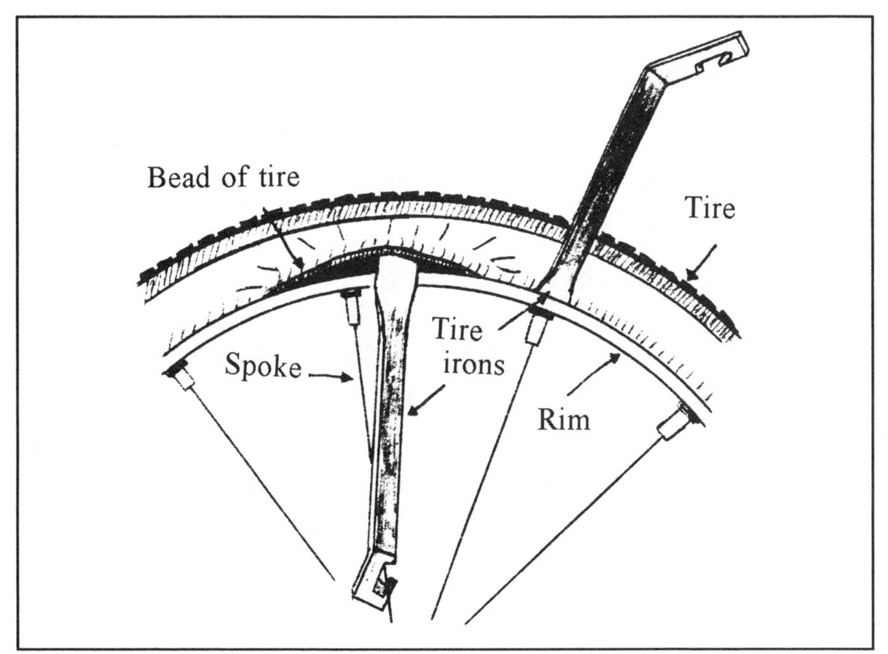

Figure 2 Using tire irons

Be careful not to pinch the tube when you do this.

STEP TWO: Hold the first tire iron in place. With the second tire iron repeat *step one*, three or four inches down the rim. Alternate tire irons, pulling the bead of the tire over the rim, section by section, until one side of the tire bead is completely off the rim.

STEP THREE: Remove the rest of the tire and tube from the rim. This can be done by hand. It's easiest to remove the valve stem last. Once the tire is off the rim, pull the tube out of the tire.

CLEAN AND SAFETY CHECK

STEP FOUR: Using a rag, wipe the inside of the tire to clean out any dirt, sand, glass, thorns, etc. These may cause the tube to puncture. The inside of a tire should feel smooth. Any pricks or bumps could mean that you have found the culprit of your flat tire and this should be checked out.

STEP FIVE: Wipe the rim clean, then check the rim strip, making sure it covers the spoke nipples properly on the inside of the rim. If a spoke is poking through the rim strip it could cause a puncture.

STEP SIX: At this point, you can do one of two things: replace the punctured tube with a new one, or patch the hole. It's easiest to simply replace the tube with a new tube if you're out on the trails. Roll up the old tube and take it home to repair later that night in front of the TV. Directions on using a patch kit are usually with the patch kit itself.

INSTALLING THE TIRE AND TUBE (This can be done entirely by hand)

STEP SEVEN: Inflate the new or repaired tube with enough air to give it shape, then tuck it back into the tire.

STEP EIGHT: To put the tire and tube back on the rim, begin by putting the valve in the valve hole. The valve must be straight. Then with your hands push the beaded edge of the tire onto the rim all the way around so that one side of your tire is on the rim.

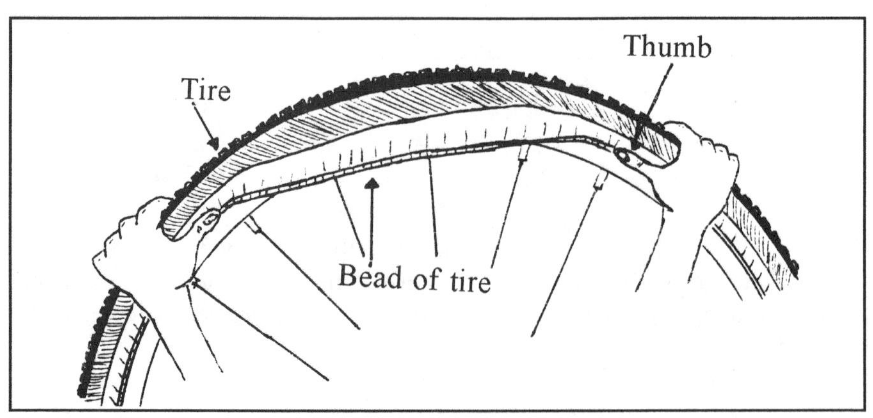

Figure 3 Wrestling a tire onto the rim

STEP NINE: Let most of the air out of the tube to allow room for the rest of the tire.

STEP TEN: Beginning opposite the valve, use your thumbs to push the other side of the tire onto the rim. Be careful not to pinch the tube in between the tire and the rim. The last few inches may be difficult, and you may need the tire iron to pry the tire onto the rim. If so, just be careful not to puncture the tube.

BEFORE INFLATING COMPLETELY

STEP ELEVEN: Check to make sure the tire is seated in the rim properly and that the tube is not caught between the tire and the rim. Do this by adding about 5 to 10 pounds of air, watching closely that the tube does not bulge out of the tire.

STEP TWELVE: Once you're sure the tire and tube are properly seated, put the wheel back on the bike, then fill the tire with air. It's easier squeezing the wheel through the brake shoes if the tire is still flat.

STEP THIRTEEN: Now fill the tire with the proper amount of air, checking constantly to make sure the tube doesn't bulge from the rim. If the tube does appear to bulge out, release all the air from the tire as quickly as you can, or you could be in for a big bang.

★ When installing the rear wheel, place the chain back onto the smallest cog (furthest gear on the right) and pull the derailleur out of the way. Your wheel should slide right on.

LUBRICATION AVOIDS DETERIORATION

Lubrication is crucial to maintaining your bike. Dry spots will be eliminated. Creaks, squeaks, grinding, and binding will be gone. The chain will run quietly and the gears will shift smoothly. The brakes will grip quicker, and your bike may last longer with less repairs. Need I say more? Well, yes. Without knowing where to put the lubrication, what good is it?

THINGS YOU WILL NEED

- One can of bicycle lubricant, found at any bike store
- A clean rag (to wipe excess lubricant from the bike)

WHAT GETS LUBRICATED

- Front derailleur
- Rear derailleur
- Shift levers
- Front brake
- Rear brake
- Both brake levers
- Chain

WHERE TO LUBRICATE

To make it simple, just spray a little lubricant on all the pivot points of your bike (if you're using a squeeze bottle, then use just a drop or two). Wherever metal moves against metal; for instance, at the center of the brake calipers, put a few drops on each point and let the lubricant sink in.

Once you have applied the lubricant to the derailleurs, shift the gears a few times, working the derailleurs back and forth. This allows the lubricant to work itself into the tiny cracks and spaces it must occupy to do its job. Work the brakes a few times as well.

LUBING THE CHAIN

Lubricating the chain should be done after the chain has been wiped clean of most road grime. Do this by spinning the chain counterclockwise (pedal backwards) while gripping the chain with a clean rag. After you're through, you will probably want to throw the rag away.

Lubricating the chain is much the same as anything else. You need to get some lubricant between each link. With an aerosol spray, just spray the chain while pedalling backwards (counterclockwise) until the chain is fully lubricated. Let the chain soak the lubricant in for a few seconds before wiping the excess off. Chains will collect dirt much faster if they have too much lubrication on them.

APPENDIX B

THE PENNSYLVANIA VEHICLE CODE
TITLE 75 CHAPTER 35

Enactment. Chapter 35 was added June 17, 1976, P.L.162, No.81.

Cross References. Chapter 35 is referred to in section 5553 of Title 42 (Judiciary and Judicial Procedure).

SUBCHAPTER A
OPERATION OF PEDALCYCLES

§ 3501. Applicability of traffic laws to pedalcycles.

(a) General rule. - Every person riding a pedalcycle upon a roadway shall be granted all of the rights and shall be subject to all of the duties applicable to the driver of a vehicle by this title, except as to special provisions in this subchapter and except as to those provisions of this title which by their nature can have no application.

(b) Application of subchapter. - The provisions of this subchapter apply whenever a pedalcycle is operated upon any highway or upon any path set aside for the exclusive use of pedalcycles subject to the exceptions stated in subsection (a).

§ 3502. Penalty for violation of subchapter.

Any person violating any provision of this subchapter is guilty of a summary offense and shall, upon conviction, be sentenced to pay a fine of $10.

§ 3503. Responsibility of parent or guardian.

The parent of any child and the guardian of any ward shall not authorize or knowingly permit the child or ward to violate any of the provisions of this title relating to the operation of pedalcycles.

§ 3504. Riding on pedalcycles.

(a) Use of seat by operator. - A person propelling a pedalcycle shall not ride other than upon or astride a permanent and regular seat attached to the pedalcycle.

(b) Number of riders. - No pedalcycle shall be used to carry more persons at one time than the number for which the pedalcycle is designed and equipped except that an adult rider may carry a child securely attached to the rider in a back pack or sling.

§ 3505. Riding on roadways and pedalcycle paths.

(a) General rule. - Except as provided in subsection (b), every person operating a pedalcycle upon a roadway shall ride as near to the right side of the roadway as practicable, exercising due care when passing a standing vehicle or one proceeding in the same direction.

(b) One-way highways. - Any person operating a pedalcycle upon a roadway of a highway, which highway carries traffic in one direction only and has two or more marked traffic lanes, may ride as near the left-hand curb or edge of the roadway as practicable, exercising due care when passing a standing vehicle or one proceeding in the same direction.

(c) Limitation on riding abreast. - Persons riding pedalcycles upon a roadway shall not ride more than two abreast except on paths or parts of roadways set aside for the exclusive use of pedalcycles.

(d) Use of available pedalcycle paths. - Whenever a lane or path for pedalcycles has been provided as part of a highway, pedalcycle riders shall use the lane or path and shall not use any other part of the highway. This subsection does not apply when use of the pedalcycle lane or path is not possible, safe or reasonable.

§ 3506. Articles carried by operator.

No person operating a pedalcycle shall carry any package, bundle or article which prevents the driver from keeping at least one hand upon the handlebars.

§ 3507. Lamps and other equipment on pedalcycles.

(a) Lamps and reflectors. - Every pedalcycle when in use between sunset and sunrise shall be equipped on the front with a lamp which emits a white light visible from a distance of at least 500 feet to the front and with a red reflector on the rear of a type approved by the department which shall be visible from all distances from 100 feet to 600 feet to the rear and with an amber reflector on each side. A lamp emitting a red light visible from a distance of 500 feet to the rear may be used in addition to the red reflector. A lamp worn by the operator of a pedalcycle shall comply with the requirements of this subsection if the lamp can be seen at the distances specified. All lamps and reflectors shall be of a type approved by the department.

(b) Audible signal devices. - A pedalcycle may be equipped with a device capable of giving a signal audible for a distance of at least 100 feet except that a pedalcycle shall not be equipped with nor shall any person use upon a pedalcycle any siren.

(c) Brakes. - Every pedalcycle shall be equipped with a braking system which will stop the pedalcycle in 15 feet from an initial speed of 15 miles per hour on a dry, level and clean pavement.

§ 3508. Pedalcycles on sidewalks and pedalcycle paths.

(a) Right-of-way to pedestrians. - A person riding a pedalcycle upon a sidewalk or pedalcycle path used by pedestrians shall yield the right-of-way to any pedestrian and shall give an audible signal before overtaking and passing a pedestrian.

(b) Business districts. - A person shall not ride a pedalcycle upon a sidewalk in a business district unless permitted by official traffic-control devices, nor when a usable pedalcycle-only lane has been provided adjacent to the sidewalk.

§ 3509. Parking.

(a) Sidewalks. -

(1) A person may park a pedalcycle on a sidewalk unless prohibited or restricted by an official traffic-control device.

(2) A pedalcycle parked on a sidewalk shall not impede the normal and reasonable movement of pedestrian or other traffic.

(b) Roadways. -

(1) A pedalcycle may be parked on the roadway at any angle to the curb or edge of the roadway at any location where parking is allowed.

(2) A pedalcycle may be parked on the roadway abreast of another pedalcycle or pedalcycles near the side of the roadway at any location where parking is allowed.

(3) A person shall not park a pedalcycle on a roadway in such a manner as to obstruct the movement of a legally parked motor vehicle.

(4) In all other respects, pedalcycles parked anywhere on a highway shall conform with the provisions of Subchapter E of Chapter 33 (relating to stopping, standing and parking).

Cross references. Section 3509 is referred to in section 3353 of this title.

APPENDIX C

ANNEX A
TITLE 25. RULES AND REGULATIONS

PART I. DEPARTMENT OF ENVIRONMENTAL RESOURCES
SUBPART B. STATE FACILITIES AND OPERATIONS
ARTICLE II. STATE FORESTS
CHAPTER 51. GENERAL PROVISIONS
(1-3, 21-24, 61-72)

Authority

The provision of this Chapter 51 issued under 1920-A of the act of April 9, 1929 (P.L. 177, No. 175) (71 P.S. § 510-20); 18 Pa. C.S. §§ 7505 and 7506, unless otherwise noted.

PRELIMINARY PROVISION

§51.1. Definitions. The following words and terms, when used in this Chapter shall have the following meanings, unless the context clearly indicates otherwise.

Bureau of Forestry - The Bureau of Forestry of the Department.

Department - The Department Environmental Resources of the Commonwealth.

District Forester - The Bureau of Forestry employee so designated.

§51.2. Scope. The provisions of this Chapter shall apply to all State Forests in the Commonwealth under the jurisdiction of the Department.

§51.3. Violations.

(a) A person is guilty of a summary offense under 18 Pa.C.S. § 7505 (relating to violation of governmental rules regarding traffic) if that person commits any act which is prohibited by § 51.21 (relating to licensed motor vehicles).

(b) A person shall be guilty of a summary offense under 18 Pa.C.S. § 7506 (relating violation of rules regarding conduct on Commonwealth property) if that person commits any act which is prohibited by any provision of this Chapter other than those set forth in subsection (a).

MOTORIZED VEHICLES

§51.21. Licensed motor vehicles. Licensed motor vehicles shall be permitted on State Forest roads open to public travel. Operation in the following manners shall be prohibited:

(1) Operation of any vehicle in a reckless or negligent manner, in excess of posted speed limits or, where no speed limit is posted, in excess of 25 miles per hour.

(2) Driving on roads, trails, or areas closed to vehicular traffic by posted signs or barriers.

(3) The use of State Forest roads for commercial purposes without a Road Use Agreement from the Department.

(4) Parking a vehicle in front of gates or on roads in such a manner as to interfere with the free use of the gate or the road.

(5) Operating unlicensed or unregistered motor vehicles on State Forest roads open to public travel.

§ 51.23. Trail bikes, off-road vehicles.

(a) Trail bikes, off-road vehicles, and all other similar motorized recreation vehicles may be operated only on designated roads, designated trails, or areas which have been designated for their use.

(b) Unless authorized in writing by the Bureau, all such vehicles are excluded from the State Forest land between September 25 and the day following the last day of antlerless deer hunting season, inclusive, as established by the Game Commission.

(c) Operation of trail bikes, off-road vehicles, and all other similar motorized recreation vehicles on any road, trail, or area not specifically designated for their use, or at any time of year in which their use excluded under this section shall be prohibited.

§ 51.24. Spark arrestors.

(a) All trail bikes, off-road vehicles, and other similar motorized recreation vehicles operating in, on, or through State Forest land shall have an approved, properly installed spark arrestor which shall meet and be qualified to either of the following:

(1) The U.S. Department of Agriculture. Forest Service Standard 5100-1a.

(2) The 80% efficiency level when determined in accordance with the appropriate SAE recommended practices J 335 or J 350 noise level restrictions.

(b) The U.S. Forest Service publication. Spark Arrestor Guide, will be used as the reference source in determining whether or not a spark arrestor is approved.

(c) Operation of any trail bike, off-road vehicle, or other similar motorized recreation vehicle in, on, or through State Forest land without an approved spark arrestor shall be prohibited.

MISCELLANEOUS PROVISIONS

§ 51.61. Camping permit. Camping without a current Camping Permit issued by the District Forester or his designee is prohibited, provided, however, that primitive backpack campers not using developed facilities shall not need a permit if they stay no more than one night at any campsite.

§51.62. Open fires.

(a) Small fires for cooking or warming purposes shall be permitted only at places where adequate precautions are taken to prevent the spread of fire into the forest. All other fires are prohibited.

(b) All open fires of any kind shall be prohibited when the forest fire danger is posted as High, Very High, or Extreme.

(c) A person causing a wildfire, in addition to possible criminal penalty, shall be liable for all damages, costs of extinction, and fines.

§ 51.63. Hunting.

(a) Hunting shall be permitted in accordance with current Pennsylvania game laws on all areas, unless otherwise posted

(b) Hunting in violation of posted closure or special restriction notices shall be prohibited.

§ 51.64. Fishing.

(a) Fishing shall be permitted in accordance with current Pennsylvania Fish Laws, unless otherwise posted.

(b) Fishing in violation of posted closure or special restriction notices is prohibited.

§ 51.65. Target shooting. Target shooting with firearms or bows and arrows at other than protected and approved targets and in conformity with the Pennsylvania Game Laws shall be prohibited.

§ 51.66. Destruction of property. Damaging, defacing, or removing any sign, structure, equipment, or other material shall be prohibited.

§ 51.67. Posting. Posting of signs without the permission of the Department shall be prohibited.

§ 51.68. Littering. Littering of areas with garbage, paper, or other waste material shall be prohibited.

§ 51.69. Swimming. Unless otherwise authorized, swimming shall be prohibited in all dams, ponds, lakes, and streams on State Forest lands.

§ 51.70. Removal of Plants. Picking, digging, cutting, damaging, or removing any living plant, vine, shrub, tree, or flower thereof shall be prohibited, unless authorized by written permit from the Department.

§ 51.71. Closure.

(a) Areas or portions of a State Forest or State Forest facilities may be closed to certain specified uses by the Department.

(b) Restricted areas of facilities will be conspicuously posted to inform the public of the restricted use of the area.

(c) Violation of the closure notices under subsection (a) shall be prohibited.

§ 51.72. Closure because of fire danger.

(a) In the event the Forest Fire danger is Very High or Extreme, the Director of the Bureau of Forestry may close all or portions of the State Forest to certain specified uses.

(b) Violation of a closure notice under subsection (a) shall be prohibited.

Local Bicycle Organizations and Interest Groups

Allen Street Athletic Club
c/o New Age Bicyclesport
Tony DeAngelo
814-234-2453
232 A W. College Avenue
State College, PA 16801
• Oriented mostly around USCF* and NORBA* racing. Has organized group mountain bike rides.

Nittany Velo Club
c/o Jerry Lauchle
814-237-7535
P.O. Box 1173
State College, PA 16804
• USCF club open to anyone interested in cycling. Includes NORBA members, road racers, and tourists.

Penn State Cycling Club
c/o Club Sports
814-865-9202
Intercollegiate Athletics
Penn State University
Room #2 I.M. Building
University Park, PA 16802
• USCF club oriented around collegiate racing. Introductory to high-competition racing through the spring season. Organized group rides daily for both on and off-road riders.

Penn State Outing Club
c/o Club Sports
814-865-9202
Intercollegiate Athletics
Penn State University
Room #2 I. M. Building
University Park, PA 16802
• The bicycle division includes mountain biking and touring for all members.

Ridge and Valley Outing CoOp
c/o Jean Aron
814-466-6067
227 Kim Port Avenue
Boalsburg, PA 16827
• A non-competitive, non-motorized community outing club of all ages. The bicycle division sponsors touring and overnight bike trips.

***USCF** (United States Cycling Federation is the national governing body for the sport of bicycle racing.)
***NORBA** (National Off-Road Bicycle Association owned by the USCF is the national governing body for the sport of off-road bicycle racing.)

STATE PARKS	Acreage	Picnicking	Camping	Fishing	Swimming	Historic Site	Skiing	Snowmobiling	Phone Numbers
Whipple Dam	244	●		●	●		●	●	814-667-3808
Greenwood Furnace	349	●	●	●	●	●	●	●	814-667-3808
Penn Roosevelt	75	●	●	●			●	●	814-667-3808
Reeds Gap	220	●	●	●	●		●	●	717-667-3622
Poe Valley	620	●	●	●	●		●	●	814-349-8778
Poe Paddy	10	●	●	●			●	●	814-349-8778
McCall Dam	8	●		●					717-966-1455
R.B. Winter	695	●	●	●	●		●	●	717-966-1455
Ravensburg	78	●	●	●					717-966-1455
Susquehanna	20	●		●					717-326-1971
Upper Pine Bottom	4	●		●					717-753-8209
Little Pine	2158	●	●	●	●	●	●	●	717-753-8209
Hyner View	6	●							717-923-O257
Hyner Run	180	●	●	●	●		●	●	717-923-O257
Kettle Creek	1626	●	●	●	●		●	●	717-923-O206
Bucktail	23013					●			814-486-3365
Black Moshannon	3481	●	●	●	●		●	●	814-342-1101
Bald Eagle	5900	●	●	●	●				814-625-2447

IMBA MEMBERSHIP APPLICATION

A non-profit, volunteer group, IMBA's goal is to keep public lands open for recreational enjoyment of responsible mountain bicyclists. We publish *Land Access Alert* as a means of keeping members informed of current issues and events. Donations above $9 are tax deductible.

ANNUAL MEMBERSHIP PRICES:

____ Basic Membership $15
____ Member of Affiliated Club 12
____ Supporting Donation 25
____ Clubs 30
____ Dealers ....60 or 150 or 1000
____ Manufacturers ....100 or 300 or 1000
____ additional donation for IMBA's programs

Canada/Mexico add $5 for mailing. Outside North America add $10 for mailing.

Name ____

Address ____

City/State/Zip _____________________________________

Phone: Home ____________________ Work ____________________

Make payment to IMBA; mail to PO Box 412043, Los Angeles, CA 90041.